CRASH
COURSE
Bass

D0101902

Printed and bound in the UK by MPG Books Ltd, Bodmin, Cornwall

Published in the UK by SMT, an imprint of Sanctuary Publishing Limited, Sanctuary House, 45-53 Sinclair Road, London W14 0NS, United Kingdom

www.sanctuarypublishing.com

All quotes kindly provided by *Bass Guitar* magazine

ISBN: 1-84492-015-1

Stuart Clayton

CONTENTS

ACKNOWLEDGEMENTS

Thanks to Kevin Beardsley for the recording, Simon Tucker for programming, Andy Rust and Cedric Lempereur at Peavey, Guy Harrop, James Millman, Bernie Goodfellow and EBS, Syd Harris, Della, Edge 'Coconut' Bullock, Pete Hughes, Keith Kerslake, Mansons, Adrian Ashton, all at *Bass Guitar* magazine and my students. And thanks also to my friends and family.

INTRODUCTION

Welcome to *Crash Course Bass*, a book written for the complete beginner who wants to start playing and make quick progress. This book comprises an eight-week course, with a lesson for each day of the week. You'll start with the absolute basics and progress from there, slowly, and hopefully without any information overload! We'll be covering all the basic aspects of bass playing along the way, as well as some simple music theory.

I'm going to assume that you're able to practise for about 45 minutes to an hour every day. This is the amount of time that I believe will be required to go over effectively what you've already learnt, as well as work on new material. I've tried to present the material here in such a way that everything can be digested in one session a day, but by all means take your time. Although this is an eight-week course, you should feel free to spend longer than a day on a section if you feel you need to, and I wouldn't recommend moving on until you're happy with everything you've covered so far. On the other hand, you may find it all a little basic and feel that you can do more. Again, that's up to you, but be careful not to bite off more than you can chew, and don't move on until you understand what you've already done. Don't feel that you have to do a lesson every day either – there may be days when you don't want to play at all, and that's fine. Sometimes a day off can be just what you need to let all the information sink in!

HOW IT WORKS

Each day I will introduce you to something new, be it a new technique, a new bassline or a new element of music theory. Many of these topics will be continuously developed over the course of the eight weeks, enabling you to have a good understanding of them at the end of the book.

This book comes with a free CD on which I've recorded all of the examples found in this book. Most of the basslines are recorded against a simple click track so that you can hear clearly how they should sound. The accompanying CD track is indicated by the CD icon next to the exercise. There will be a new bassline or 'practical exercise' on most days.

Some of the exercises are tougher than others. In these cases you'll see the weight-lifter symbol next to the exercise. You'll probably find that you need to spend more time on these exercises. From week 3 onwards, I'll be introducing a 'core topic' each week, each topic focusing on a different style of music, with basslines to learn that represent this style. Many of these will be a little more difficult than the previous exercises, so don't be surprised to see the weight-lifter icon cropping up more often!

All of the basslines in the core-topic chapters are recorded in the 'music minus one' format – that is, they're played twice, but the second time around the recorded

bass drops out, giving you the chance to play along with the backing track. All of these tracks have full backing tracks, allowing you to get more of a feel of playing in a band situation. These tracks are indicated by the icon shown here.

On many days there will be two types of exercise: study exercises and practical exercises. You should take as much time as you need over the study exercises since many of the concepts presented in them will need time to sink in. For the practical exercises, I've made recommendations as to how long I think they should take. Most exercises will have either 15- or 30-minute targets, although you shouldn't worry if they take longer.

In some chapters I will suggest listening to famous recordings by well-known artists. Doing so will help you to understand the material better.

In some chapters you may find that I've highlighted a certain piece of information and added the exclamation point icon. This means that it's a particularly important or useful piece of information. Note that I will also highlight important words with *italics*.

At the end of each week there will be a larger test, covering everything you studied over the previous seven days. If you struggle with this, I would advise going back over the material and taking the test again before moving on. Each test day contains a timed exercise, and these will get progressively harder as you work through the book.

On many of the days throughout this book I have added quotes from famous players. Many of these will be relevant to the study topic of the day, but others will be simple pearls of wisdom that are good advice for any player.

My final words for today are 'good luck'. I honestly believe that, with enough determination and practice, anyone can learn to play the bass. I hope that this book helps you to get started!

Stuart Clayton

October 2003

GETTING STARTED

Before we can begin playing, we need to look at a few basic concepts. The first of these is how to read music. Throughout the course of this book I will be gradually showing you how to read actual musical notation. Reading music is a complicated process, with a steep learning curve, and this book will serve as merely a brief introduction to it. So in order for you to be able to understand the exercises in the coming pages, I have also presented them in tablature, or *tab*, as it's commonly known. Tab is a very popular method of writing and reading guitar/bass music that requires only a small amount of study in order to get started. In this section, I am going to introduce you to tab so that you can get started straight away.

Before you can read tab, however, you need to know the names of the strings on your bass. From lowest to highest these are E, A, D and G. You can see these labelled in the diagram below:

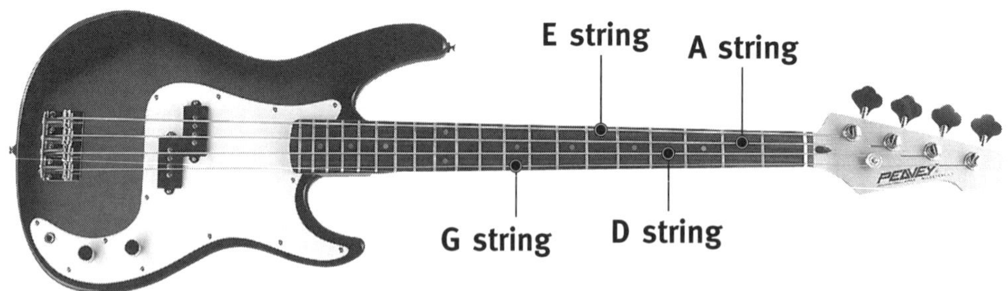

If you have a five-string bass (which I don't recommend for beginners), you'll have an extra string, situated above the E string and tuned to a low B. Therefore the strings on a five-string will be tuned to B, E, A, D and G.

TABLATURE

As you'll see in the diagram on the right, on a tab stave there are four lines, each representing a string on the bass. At the top is G, and at the bottom is E. The numbers written on these lines relate to which fret you should play. Therefore, as in the example below, if a number 7 appeared on the bottom line, followed by a 5 on the next line, you would play the seventh fret on the E string, followed by the fifth fret on the A string. Tab is read from left to right, just as you would read a book. It's that simple!

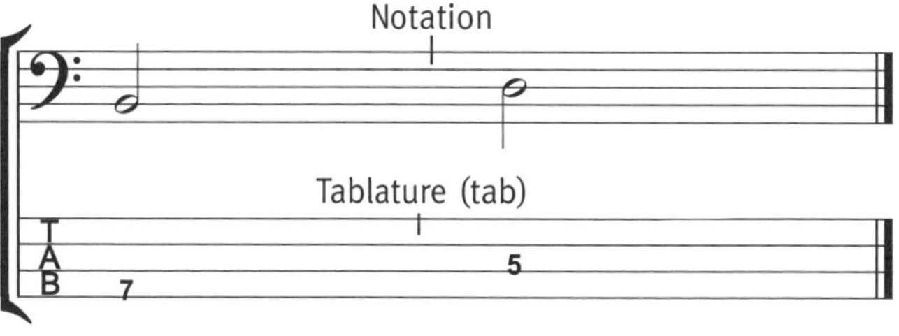

Any notes that are to be played together, such as the notes in a chord, would be stacked vertically, like this:

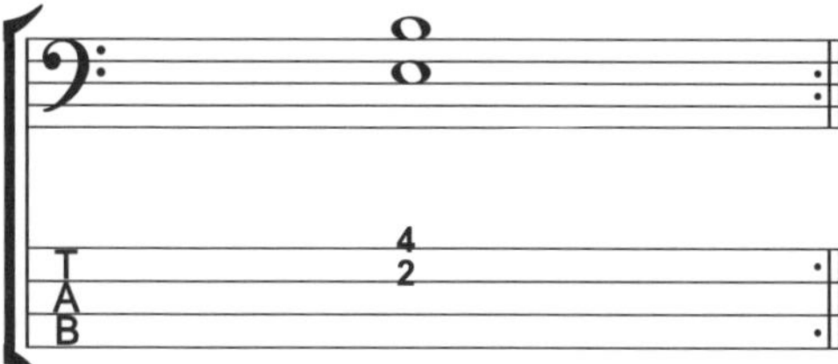

We'll begin looking at the basics of music notation on Day 3. You'll be glad to hear that you don't need to worry about it too much for now!

Bass

HOW TO PRACTISE

As I've already said, you'll need to practise every day in order to improve on the bass. But before you dive in, let's be sure that you understand how best to go about practising.

In the photographs below, you can see how to hold the bass correctly in both sitting and standing positions. You may notice from the photographs that the bass remains in roughly the same place whether standing or sitting. This can be achieved by adjusting your strap length so that the bass isn't too low on your body when you're standing. The benefits of these playing positions mean that the angles in your arms don't change drastically when you stand up to play, which in turn means that what you learn in your lessons you should then be able to use when performing. I recommend doing most of your practice whilst sitting, since you'll be more comfortable this way.

Playing whilte standing...

...or sitting

CREATING A PRACTICE SCHEDULE

Practising is funny thing – some people love it, some hate it. Either way, I'm afraid you need to do it! But a common mistake for musicians is to practise for hours one day then not at all for the next few days. This doesn't work. It's infinitely better to play for an hour every day. Progress on any instrument is best achieved in small, daily steps. With this in mind, it makes sense to have some kind of practice schedule. In the early days, this will be more difficult and you might not feel you know enough to spend an hour practising. However, as the days go by, you'll gradually develop your playing skills – and you'll need to keep practising them.

YOUR ENVIRONMENT

Try to find a quiet place in which to practise. This will need to be a small area where you can sit and work uninterrupted for an hour a day. Try to have everything you need – pens, paper, CD player, amplifier, tuner, leads, etc – to hand, as this will make life easier.

WARMING UP

Once you've started playing a little more regularly, you'll need to think about warming up on the bass. Each time you sit down to play, you should work through a few simple exercises that will prepare your fingers. These exercises are introduced on Day 5, and while they're quite simple, they are excellent devices for warming up. In the mean time, you can warm up by playing lightly on your instrument.

With the basics now out of the way, it's time to get started on your crash course!

WEEK 1

OVERVIEW

In this first week we're going to be looking at the absolute basics of beginning to play the bass guitar. Here's a full breakdown of what we'll be covering over the course of the coming week:

- **An Introduction To Bass Guitar** – You need to be familiar with the various features of the bass guitar. This week we'll look at what they are and what they do.

- **Tuning Up** – You won't get far with an out-of-tune bass, so one of the first things we'll look at is how to tune up.

- **Music Notation** – Our first step in looking at notated music will be to examine the stave and bass clef. You'll also learn where the open-string notes are written on the stave.

- **Fretboard Knowledge** – We'll be learning the names of the notes at the fifth, seventh and twelfth frets.

- **Basic Technique** – In order to prevent you from picking up bad playing habits, we'll look at the fundamentals of right- and left-hand technique from the start.

- **Practical Exercises** – Finally, and most importantly, we'll learn some simple basslines!

DAY 1: AN INTRODUCTION TO THE BASS GUITAR

Your goals for Day 1 are:

- To remember the names and functions of the various features on the bass;
- To learn your first bassline.

QUOTE FOR THE DAY

Don't ever underestimate the four-string Fender bass.

– John Giblin

Without doubt, the first step on your path towards being a bass player is to become familiar with the instrument. I'm assuming here that you know either nothing or very little about the bass – so if you already have some basic knowledge, this will be an easy lesson for you! There are many different kinds of bass guitar, and many different manufacturers, but all of the instrument's features shown on the next page remain constant from bass to bass.

In the illustration over the page you can see a standard four-string bass guitar, with the key features on the instrument numbered. I suggest that you read through this information and digest it as thoroughly as you can – you'll find that most of these features have very elementary names. You should then examine your own bass guitar and find all of these features on it. Try to remember them – I'll be referring to them throughout the course of the book, so you'll need to be familiar with them.

Bass

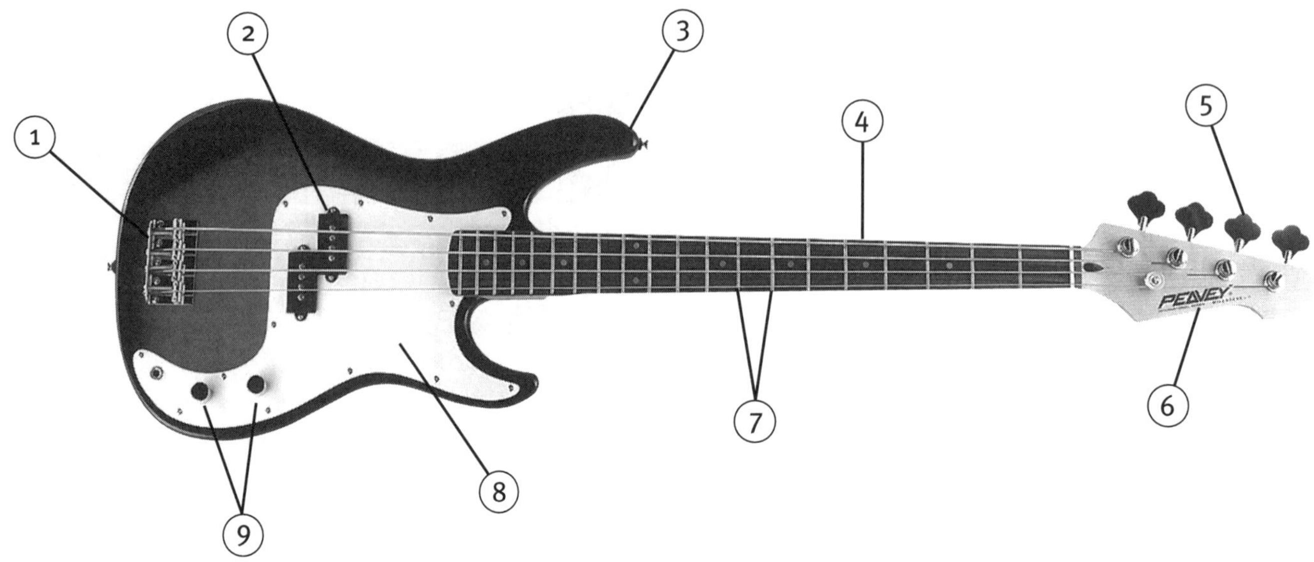

(1) The *bridge*. This is the place where the strings are anchored and adjustments are made to the string height.

(2) These are the *pickups*. You'll notice that this bass has two, although some basses may have only one. These pick up the sound you make and send it to the amplifier.

(3) The *strap button*. This is where you connect the strap. You can see the second strap button at the body end of the bass, to the left of the bridge.

(4) The *neck*.

(5) The *tuning pegs*.

(6) The *headstock*.

(7) The *frets*. These divide the fretboard into individual notes.

(8) The *body*. This is the main section of the bass and is made out of wood.

(9) The *controls*. These vary greatly from bass to bass, but on each model they control the instrument's volume and tone.

AMPLIFICATION

Although it's possible to practise the bass acoustically, it's nevertheless a good idea to have some kind of amplifier to play through. Bass amplifiers come in two basic varieties: combo and stack. A combo is literally a combination of an amplifier and speaker housed in the same case, while a stack is a separate amplifier and speaker used together. For beginners, a combo will be more than sufficient, and it's possible to pick up a small bass combo for around £90–£100 ($140–$155). A stack will be considerably more expensive.

Combos

Stack

PRACTICAL EXERCISE

I couldn't let you end your first lesson without leaving you with something to play now could I? Below is a very simple bassline. (It's also the first bassline I ever leant to play!) You'll have to follow the tab for this one. If in doubt, go back and re-read the notes on reading tab in the 'Getting Started' section at the beginning of the book. The line is also on the CD for you to hear.

Exercise 1

DAY 1 STUDY

1 After studying the illustration on page 18, see if you can name all of the features on your bass. I would suggest having someone test you. Remember that most have very self-explanatory names.

2 What is the difference between a stack and a combo?

3 Practise your first bassline!

DAY 2: TUNING UP!

Your goals for Day 2 are:

- To learn how to tune your bass;
- To learn two more simple basslines.

When learning the bass, and indeed any musical instrument, there are certain things you need to get right from the start. One that's right near the top of that list is *tuning*. It is vital to be in tune, since playing while out of tune is a bad influence on your ears – and on the ears of anyone who can hear you practising! Therefore, today, we will look at how to tune your bass. We'll also look at some simple basslines. There are a few different methods for tuning up, and which one you use is your own preference. However, at this early stage I'm just going to show you the simplest method. We'll look at the other methods in a later week.

First of all, you'll need to tune to a *reference pitch*. What I mean by this is that you need to tune to something that's already in tune – otherwise, you run the risk of your bass being in tune with itself but not with anything else! I believe it's important to get the top string, the G, in tune first, and then tune the other strings from there. To that end, you'll find a G reference pitch on the CD. Once you have the G string in tune, you can tune the rest of the strings by what's known as *relative*

tuning. To begin, play the open G string, followed by the D string at the fifth fret. This note is also a G, and the two should be identical. It not, listen closely and see if you can discern whether the second note is too sharp or too flat, then adjust it accordingly. Don't worry if it takes you a few goes to get it right.

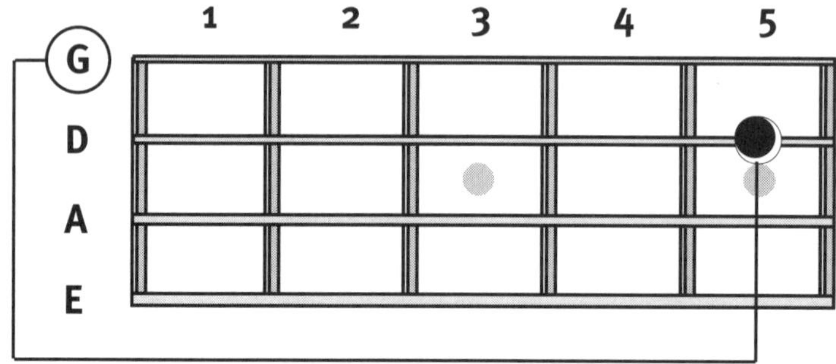

Once you're happy that your D string is also in tune, you can use the same method to tune the A string. The open D string should sound the same as the fifth fret of the A string:

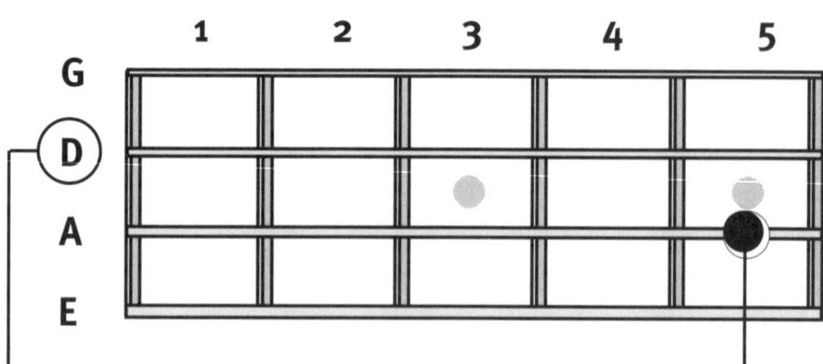

Finally, repeat the process with the open A string and the fifth fret of the E string. Again, they both need to be the same.

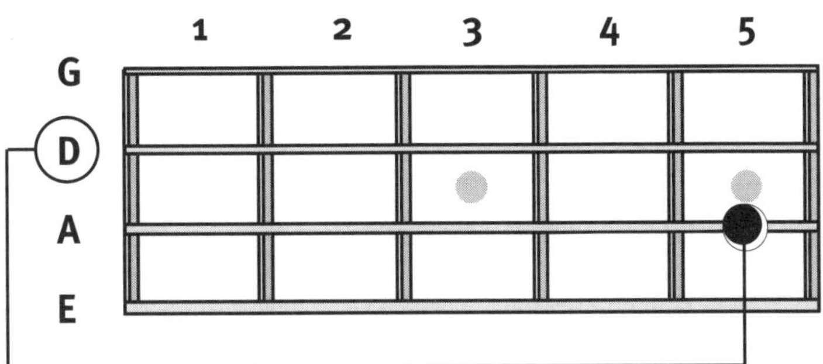

Bear in mind that you need to be as accurate as possible when tuning each string. If you tune inaccurately – even slightly – on the first pair of notes, the error will multiply as you tune the other strings.

PRACTICAL EXERCISE

The second part of today's lesson is a little more practical. Below I've written out a couple of simple bass parts. By using the tab and by listening to the CD, you should be able to play these, with a little practice.

Exercise 2

Bass

Exercise 3

DAY 2 STUDY

1 Practise tuning the bass using the G reference pitch on the CD. Remember to be as accurate as possible – try to do this every time you play.

2 Practise the two basslines that you learnt this week.

Bass

DAY 3: AN INTRODUCTION TO MUSIC NOTATION

Your goals for Day 3 are:

- To understand some of the basics of music notation;
- To learn two new basslines.

QUOTE FOR THE DAY

It's nice to be able to write things. All those early songs are written down. Even things like Cream's 'White Room' were actually scored.

– Jack Bruce, Cream

In this book, as with most guitar music books, the material is presented in both standard notation and tablature. You were introduced to tab in 'Getting Started', but now it's time to take a look at the fundamentals of music notation. Don't be scared!

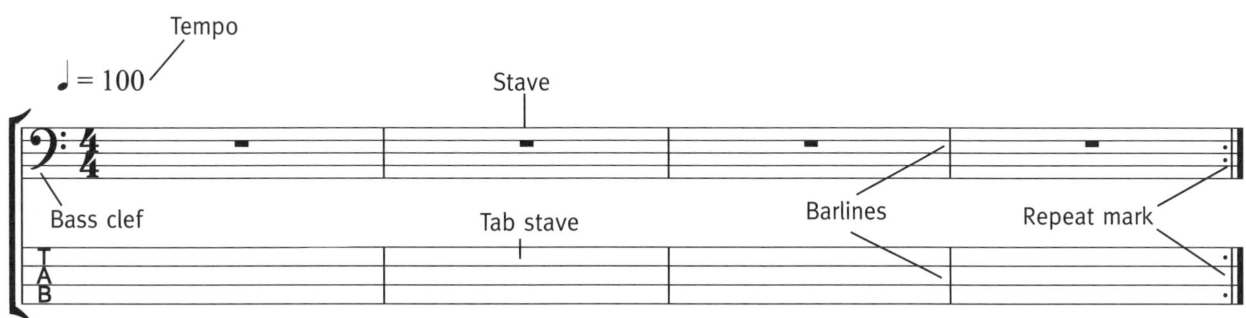

THE BASS CLEF

The *bass clef* is the symbol that appears at the beginning of each line of music and tells us that we're in the *bass register*. This means that the notes that we play are going to sound lower than those played by a guitar, trumpet or any other higher-pitched instrument. On the bass clef, each line and space represents a note, and today I'm going to show you where the open strings of your bass are written on the bass clef. Remember where these notes are. In the coming days, we'll be looking at the locations of the other notes on the bass clef.

THE STAVE

Look at any music book and you'll see that music notation – whether it be for bass, piano, guitar or any other instrument – is written on a series of five horizontal lines. This is called the *stave*.

BARLINES

You may also notice that the stave is separated into smaller sections by vertical lines. These divide the music up into *bars*, and not surprisingly these lines are known as *barlines*. Most Western music is in what's known as *4/4 time*, or *common time* (sometimes written as just the letter **C**), meaning that there are four beats in a bar. You can think of a beat as a foot-tap; by tapping your foot in time to a piece of music, you're marking out the beats.

REPEAT MARK

This double line with two dots before it is a repeat mark. This means that you should go back to the beginning and play through the exercise again.

TEMPO

At the beginning of each example in this book, you will see a *tempo* mark. This tells you the speed of the exercise in *beats per minute*. You should always practise to something that will give you accurate time, be it a drum machine or a metronome. Metronomes come in both mechanical and electronic varieties and are available from all good music shops.

You'll need to remember all of these terms, as they'll be referred to over the coming weeks.

PRACTICAL EXERCISE

A bass lesson wouldn't be complete without a new practical exercise for you to study! Over the page is another simple bassline for you to get your teeth into. This one is a little tougher than the previous ones, so keep an eye on the tab and listen to the CD for guidance.

Bass

Exercise 4

DAY 3 STUDY

1 Remember the names of the music notation elements we looked at this week.

2 Find some music paper and practise drawing a bass clef and writing the four notes that you've just learnt: E, A, D and G. At the back of this book there are some pages of empty staves for you to doodle on.

3 Study a music book containing your favourite songs. Have a look at how the music is written.

4 Practise your new basslines. Be sure to keep practising the lines you've learned on previous days as well!

DAY 4: RIGHT HAND TECHNIQUE

Your goals for Day 4 are:

- To understand and practise basic right hand technique;
- To learn two new basslines.

Before you start playing too much, we need to look at how you're going to attack the strings. For now, I'm going to assume that you're playing with your fingers rather than a pick, although pick playing will be covered in a later week. It can be quite tricky to play *fingerstyle* to begin with, and it's very important to get the technique right from the beginning, as poor technique at this stage can be difficult to correct afterwards. To begin, place the thumb of your right hand on the pickup as shown in the photograph below. This gives you somewhere to anchor the hand so that it's not left floating in mid-air. Now, play the E string with your first and second fingers. (It doesn't matter which you start with, but be sure to alternate them continuously.)

Bass

Try to maintain a smooth angle in your fingers – don't bend them too much at the knuckles. As you can see in the photograph, my fingers are gently curved so that the tip of my finger plucks the strings.

Whatever you're playing, try to keep an eye on your right hand and make sure that you're continuously alternating fingers.

PRACTICAL EXERCISE

To finish off today's lesson, here are two new basslines to practise. Take them slowly, and remember to refer to the CD.

Exercise 5

Exercise 6

DAY 4 STUDY

1 Be sure you understand the right-hand technique described this week. Try to apply it to everything you play from now on.

2 Practise your two new basslines.

DAY 5: LEFT HAND TECHNIQUE

Your goals for Day 5 are:

- To understand and practise basic left-hand technique;
- To learn a new simple bassline.

QUOTE FOR THE DAY

You cannot practise without practice.

– Jeff Berlin

LEFT HAND TECHNIQUE

Believe it or not, the left hand requires just as much attention as the right. In this section we're going to look at an exercise designed to help you train your left-hand fingers. If practised every day, this exercise will help you to gain dexterity and independence in each finger, something that's very important for a bass player. It also makes a good warm-up exercise – and, as I said in the 'Getting Started' section, you should always warm up before you play!

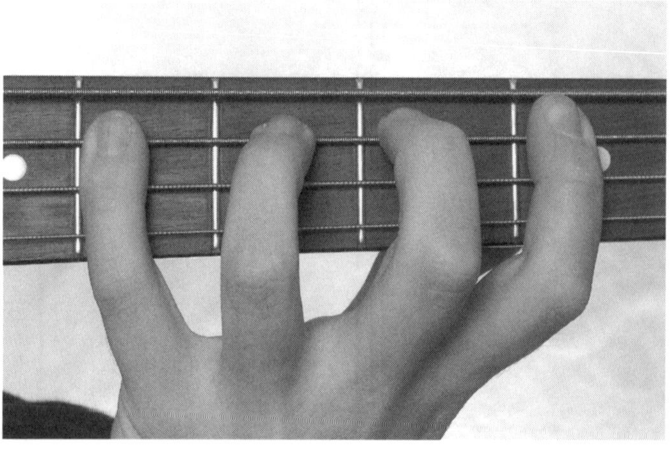

You have four fingers on your left hand, and it makes sense to use them all. The following exercise is based on a system that I call the *finger-per-fret system*. Since this exercise is concentrated within the first four frets, it makes sense to use a finger on each. Throughout this exercise you should aim to play with your fingertips in the centre of the fret. You may have noticed that the closer you get to the frets themselves, the more excess noise, or 'fret buzz', you get. You should aim to avoid noises like this at all times, so try to keep your finger position central. Try also to keep your hand in a relaxed position, with the thumb at the back of the neck (not coming over the top of the fretboard), and maintain a smooth curve in your fretting fingers. Take a look at the photograph on the previous page for an example of good hand positioning.

Exercise 7

Listen to this example on the CD and pay attention to how it sounds – clean and smooth, with no excess noise. You should aim for the same accuracy. Be aware that this is a slow exercise – there's nothing to be gained from playing it too fast, so stick to the tempo indicated. Also, make sure that you're still alternating your right-hand plucking fingers, as discussed earlier. Exercises like this make great warm-ups, so remember to play through this one every time you sit down to play.

Bass

You might find this exercise a bit of a stretch, starting down at the first fret. If your hands aren't big or flexible enough to stretch like this, you can start the exercise at the fifth fret instead. Try to move back down to the first fret when your fingers are more accustomed to the exercise.

PRACTICAL EXERCISE

Here is today's bassline for you to study.

Exercise 8

DAY 5 STUDY

1 Remember that you need to warm up. Play the left-hand exercise shown above every time you practise.

2 Practise your new bassline.

DAY 6: WHAT ARE ALL THESE NOTES?

Your goals for Day 6 are:

- To learn the names of the notes at the fifth, seventh and twelfth frets;
- To learn two more simple bass parts.

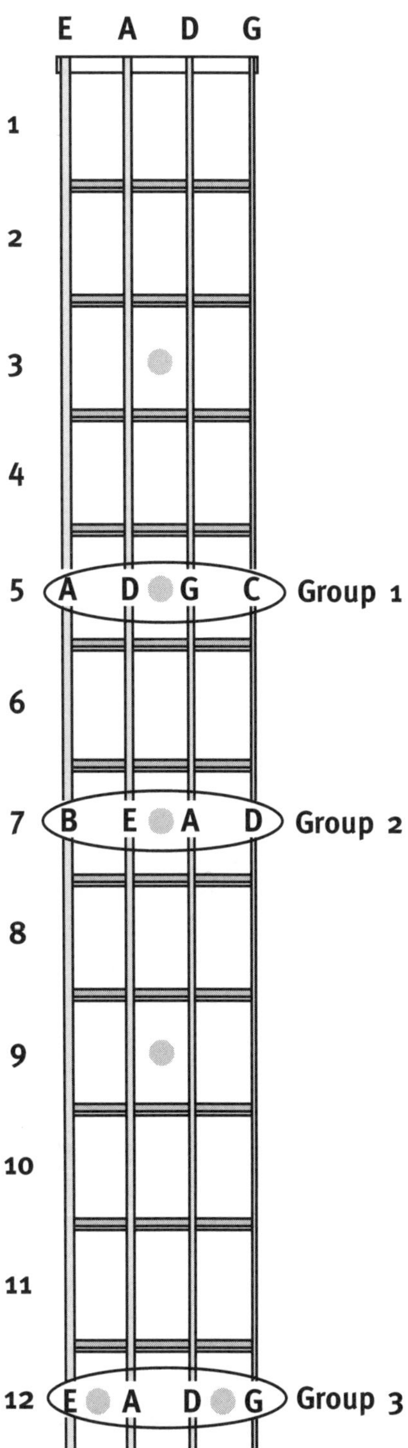

If you've got this far, you'll have been introduced to the bass guitar and have even learnt to play a couple of simple bass parts on it. Not bad for a few days' work! But I bet part of you is looking at that fretboard and feeling quite daunted – after all, there are a lot of notes on there! One of the most important things to address in the early stages of your playing is to learn what those notes are. The more you know about your fretboard, the more you can do with it – it's as simple as that. The important thing is not to be put off by the sheer number of notes on the bass. I can tell you straight away that there is an enormous amount of repetition – after all, there are only 12 actual notes, right? What we're going to do today is look at some of the easier notes to remember. Believe it or not, we're actually going to cover about 12 notes today, and you shouldn't have too much difficulty remembering them.

In the diagram opposite, you'll see an illustration of the neck of your bass guitar. Note that it only goes as far as the 12th fret, since after

that everything is repeated. As you can see, I've marked on the illustration the names of the notes we are going to learn. Let's divide them up into groups.

GROUP 1: THE FIFTH FRET

Some of these notes should be familiar to you from your tuning-up exercise from Day 4. You should know, for instance, that the fifth fret on the D string is a G, just like the open G string. In fact, the only one you won't know is the fifth fret of the G string – this is a C. So the notes we have at the fifth fret are A, D, G and C.

GROUP 2: THE SEVENTH FRET

Like all of the notes we'll cover this week, you'll see that these are all natural – there are no sharps or flats involved. You might also notice that reading across the fret spells the word 'BEAD', which may help you to remember them in these early stages! Hopefully you can also see the pattern of E, A and D at the same fret on adjacent strings – this is the same sequence as your open strings. Try to look out for these patterns; there are many of them, and it's very useful to able to spot them.

GROUP 3: THE TWELFTH FRET

This is the easiest group of the lot, since we're at the octave fret. This means that each note is the same as the open string, but an octave higher – E, A, D and G. Easy!

Do your best to memorise these notes. I can't stress enough how important it is to know them. Hopefully, since we'll be taking them in small steps, you should find it easy to commit them to memory.

The remaining notes on the bass will be covered in the days ahead in the 'Notebuster' sections.

DAY 6 STUDY

1 What notes are found at the fifth fret of the bass?

2 Which notes are found at the seventh fret?

3 Which notes are found at the twelfth fret?

4 Be sure be practise everything you've learnt so far. Tomorrow is the first big test day!

Bass

DAY 7

WEEK 1 TEST

Congratulations on getting to the end of the first week. It's now time to test you on what you've learnt so far. This set of questions and practical exercises covers what you have learnt in your first week. You should complete this test before moving on to the next section. Good luck!

QUOTE FOR THE DAY

If you get bogged down with something you're trying to learn, and you're not getting it, then leave it alone for a couple of days and come back and you'll probably find you'll come back much better.

– Steve Harris, Iron Maiden

1 On this illustration of a bass guitar, add the names of the numbered features:

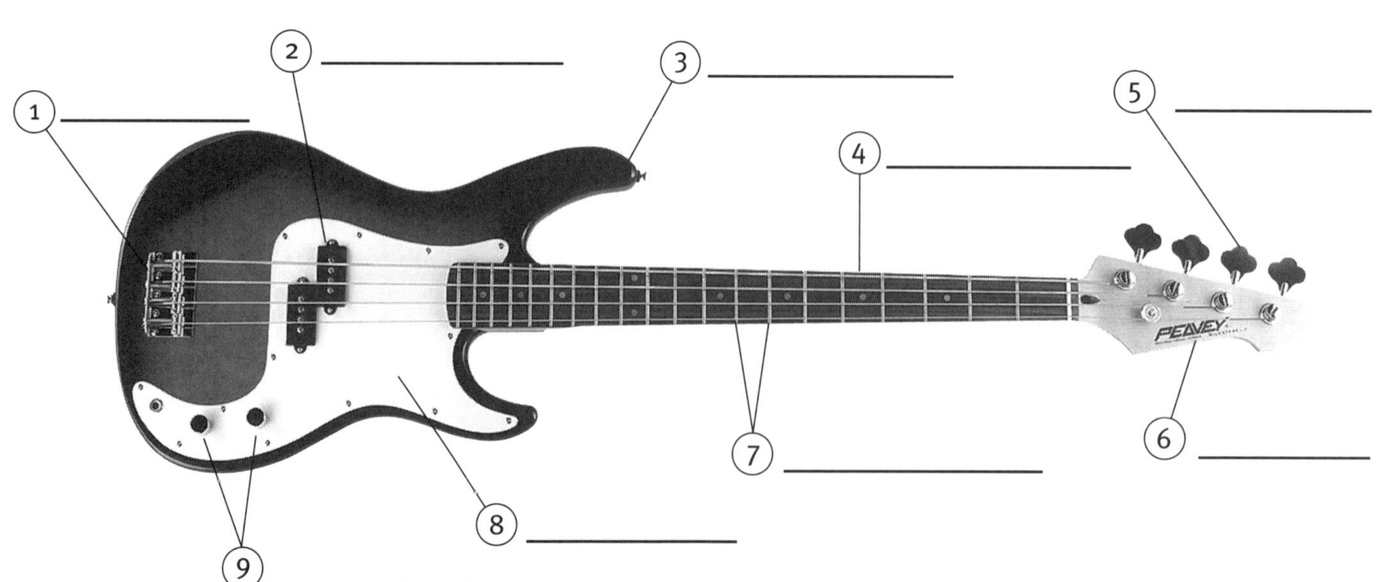

2 Why is it so important to tune to a reference pitch?

3 What is the bass clef and what does it mean?

4 Write the open-string notes on this stave:

5 Which note is found at the seventh fret of the D string?

6 Which note is found at the fifth fret of the A string?

7 Which note is found at the twelfth fret of the E string?

8 How else might 4/4 time be written?

9 What are the vertical lines that divide up the stave into bars called?

10 What are the benefits of the finger-per-fret approach?

Bass

Finally, here's a new bassline for you to study. You should aim to be able to play this one within 15 minutes.

WEEK 2

OVERVIEW

Now that you've been introduced to some of the fundamentals, we're going to develop what you've learnt and introduce a few new topics. Here's a full breakdown of what we'll cover in the following week:

- **Left Hand Technique** – We'll be expanding on what you learnt in the first week with two new left-hand dexterity exercises.
- **Right Hand Technique** – We're also going to develop your right hand further with something I call the 'travelling thumb' technique.
- **Fretboard Knowledge** – This week we're going to cover the notes at the first, third, ninth and tenth frets.
- **Octaves** – These are a useful tool for any bassist, and this week we'll be looking at what they are and how to use them.
- **Music Notation** – This week we'll look at the positions of the other notes on the stave, as well as our first rhythmic value: the quarter note.
- **Practical Exercises** – And, of course, we'll also be looking at some more basslines!

DAY 8: DEVELOPING THE LEFT HAND

Your goals for Day 8 are:

- To learn a new left-hand exercise;
- To learn the notes at the third fret;
- To learn a new bassline.

LEFT HAND EXERCISES

Back on Day 5 we began to look at some left-hand exercises designed to give your left-hand fingers a bit of a workout and encourage smoother playing. We're going to expand on this now, with a longer, extended exercise. This new exercise will use more of the fretboard, but the finger-per-fret approach will remain. As with the previous left-hand exercise, this isn't meant to be played fast, so stick to the specified tempo (60bpm) and remember to keep all notes long and smooth and maintain an even volume across all four strings. Be sure that each finger stays in the centre of the fret in order to avoid any unwanted fret buzz.

PRACTICAL EXERCISE

This exercise is one that I refer to as 'The Snake' because of its zigzag motion across the fretboard. You'll see what I mean when you play it!

Exercise 9

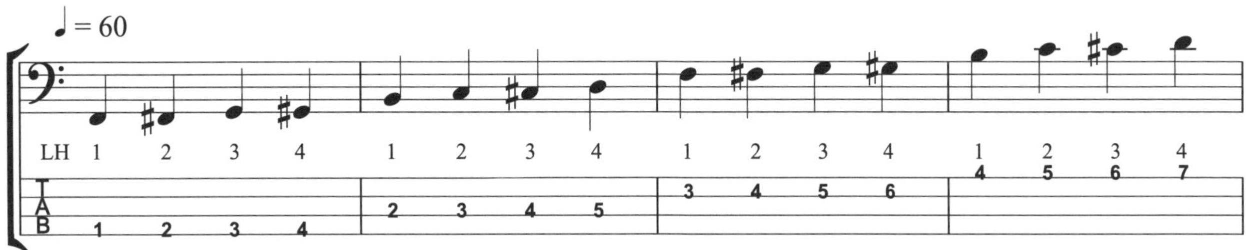

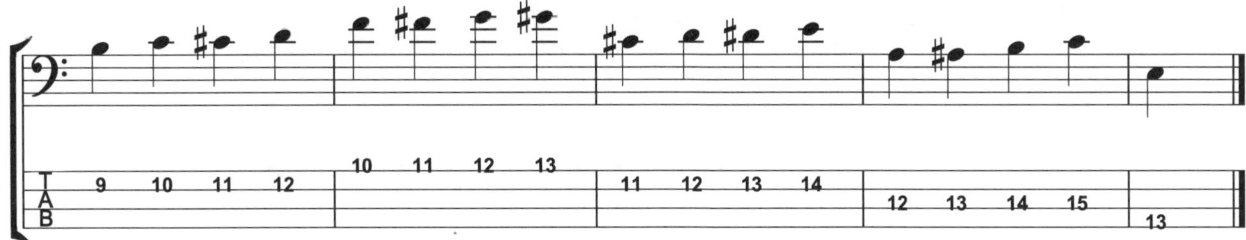

Exercises such as this one are very important to build up your hand strength in these early days.

Bass

NOTEBUSTER: THE THIRD FRET

It's time to learn a few more notes. Today we are going to look at those found at the third fret. Take a look at the illustration opposite.

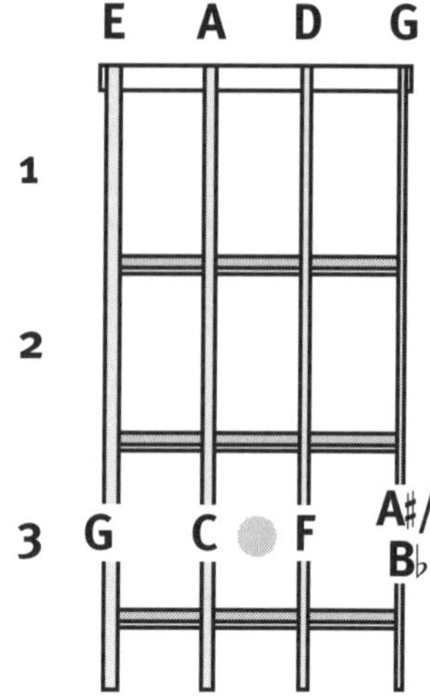

Like all of the notes we've looked at so far, you'll see that most of the notes at the third fret are also natural – with the exception of the one found on the G string. This note can be referred to as either A♯ or B♭, and it's what we call an *accidental*. Add these notes to the ones you learnt last week, and you should see that already we have covered quite a few – and hopefully without too much difficulty!

PRACTICAL EXERCISE

Today's exercise will require you to use the finger-per-fret technique.

DAY 8 STUDY

1. Get someone to test you randomly on the notes you know on the fretboard. You'll find many of the coming exercises easier if you have good fretboard knowledge.

2. Add 'The Snake' exercise to your daily warm-up routine.

3. Practise today's Practical Exercise.

DAY 9: INTRODUCING THE OCTAVE

Your goals for Day 9 are:

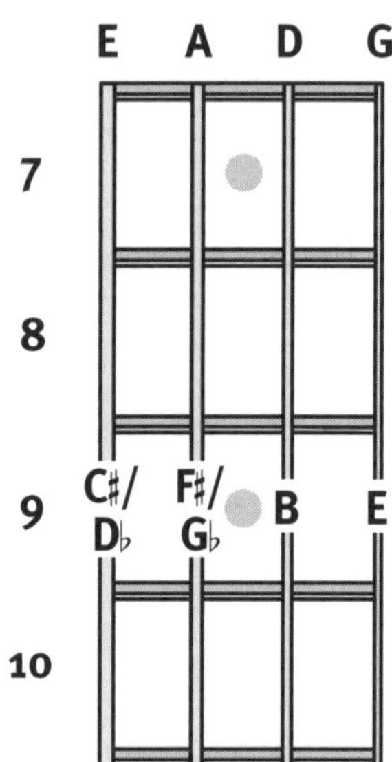

The ninth fret

- To learn the notes at the ninth fret;
- To learn about octaves and play two simple basslines using them.

NOTEBUSTER: THE NINTH FRET

You might have noticed that all of the frets we've looked at so far have been ones labelled with position markers, or dots. There's now only one of these frets left to look at: the ninth fret. Here, as at the third fret, we're going to encounter a sharp/flat note – in fact, two of them. As you'll see in the diagram above, the note found at the ninth fret of the E string is a C♯, or D♭, and the note at the ninth fret of the A string is an F♯, or G♭. The other two notes are naturals: a B and E for the D and G strings respectively. You might have noticed that there was also a B and an E at the seventh fret of the E and A strings – another pattern emerging! Our new notes are an octave above these lower ones. Confused? Don't worry – octaves are explained in detail over the page.

OCTAVES

We've just briefly mentioned octaves. Now it's time to learn a little more about them and, more importantly, how to play and use them. As a bass player, octaves are one of your best friends – they work for any kind of bass part, they sound great and they can help you find your way around the fingerboard. By understanding octaves and combining that understanding with the fretboard knowledge you've acquired so far, you should begin to see more patterns on the neck of the bass. But before we start playing anything, some of you may be wondering what an octave is. An octave is the distance from one note to the next note with the same name – the distance from C to the next C, for example. This is shown on the keyboard diagram below:

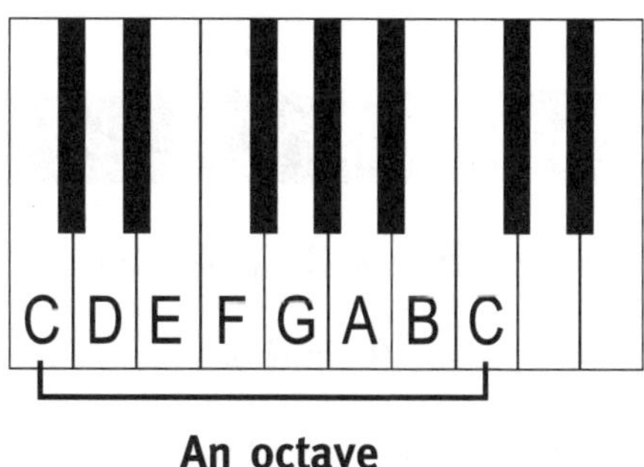

An octave

Now let's play this same octave on the bass. Play the C at the third fret of the A string (I suggest fretting the note with the first finger of your left hand), then play the C at the fifth fret of the G string. Fret this one with either your third or fourth finger, and keep your hand in position so that you can play one followed by the other.

Bass

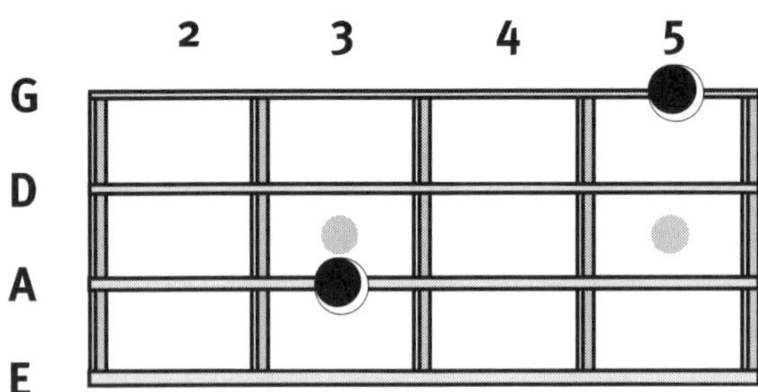

You can find the octave of any note by going along two frets, then across two strings, as show in the diagram above. This shape is completely moveable and will always enable you to play an octave. For example we could move it so that you were playing the eighth fret of the A string (an F) and the tenth fret of the G string (also an F). You can hear this on the CD. Note that this formula will work only on the E and A strings, since there won't be enough strings on the bass to use it from the D or G!

PRACTICAL EXERCISE

Now let's look at a couple of simple basslines that incorporate octaves. As with all these basslines, study them thoroughly first and be sure you understand the material. They're a little more difficult than the previous exercises, but you should be able to play them with some practice. Again, refer to the CD if you need to.

Exercise 11

Exercise 12

DAY 9 STUDY

1 Which notes are found at the ninth fret of the bass? (Have someone test you on this, and on all the previous ones as well.)

2 Practise playing octaves at various points all over the bass.

3 Practise the octave-based practical exercises covered in this chapter.

Bass

DAY 10: QUARTER NOTES

Your goals for Day 10 are:

- To recognise and be able to write C on the bass clef;
- To understand quarter notes and learn some basslines based on them.

QUOTE FOR THE DAY

My main focus is playing in the pocket. A solid pocket is what I find most people appreciate about a great bassist.

– Nathan East

Back on Day 3 I introduced you the basics of music notation – the bass clef, barlines and the stave. It's time now to start putting some notes onto that stave and learning how to read them. You'll recall that we've already learnt four notes: the E, A, D and G that represent our open strings. Be aware that some of these notes can also be played at the fifth fret. Today we're going to learn a new note: C.

The C found at the third fret of the A string is written in the second space up from the bottom of the stave. The C found an octave above is also important, so below I've written both Cs on the stave. Try to remember them.

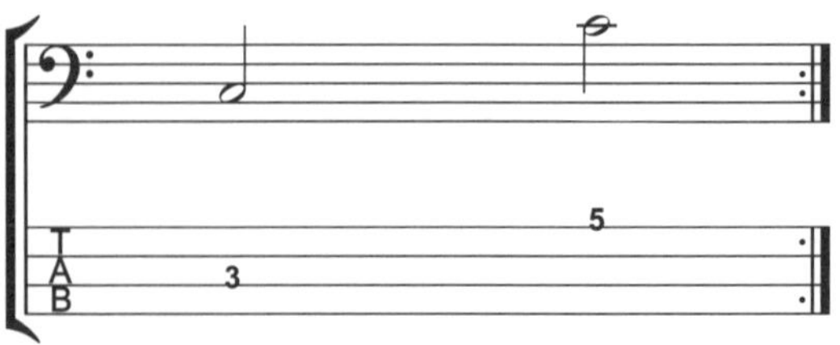

You now have five notes to recognise on the stave.

RHYTHMS

Before we look at quarter notes, I want you to study the following chart, which illustrates all of the basic note values and their respective rests. You'll also be able to see the differing UK and US terminologies. Bizarrely, I think the US names make more sense. We'll be studying each of these rhythms individually over the coming weeks, and you should use this chart as a reference in the mean time.

UK Terms	US Terms	Note	Rest	Duration	In Use
Semibreve	Whole note			4 beats	
Minim	Half note			2 beats	
Crotchet	Quarter note			1 beat	
Quaver	Eighth note			1/2 beat	
Semiquaver	16th note			1/4 beat	

QUARTER NOTES

Quarter notes are represented in time signatures by the number 4. In 4/4 time we therefore have room for four quarter notes in a bar. You can also think of this as one note on each beat. In order for you to hear these in action, I've prepared some simple bass parts using just quarter notes, with the beat numbers written below each exercise. You'll need to look closely at the music notation for the next few exercises as tab doesn't contain any rhythmic information. (Indeed, this is the main disadvantage of tab.) You should use the tab only to help you find the note positions.

Bass

Exercise 13

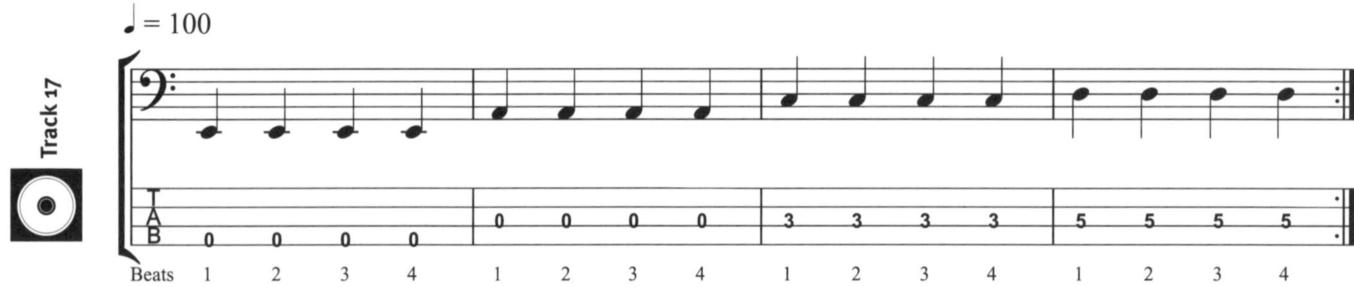

You will also need to become familiar with the quarter-note rest, which you can see in the chart above. Here's another bass part which makes use of the quarter-note rest. As always, refer to the CD if you need to.

Exercise 14

Don't be put off by these exercises. At this early stage you're not expected to 'sight-read' these parts, just to study them and become familiar with the concepts involved.

DAY 10 STUDY

1 Practise reading quarter-note bass parts. Try to look at the notation as well as the tab.

2 Look through some printed music and look out for quarter notes and their rests.

DAY 11: A NEW LEFT HAND EXERCISE

Your goals for Day 11 are:

- To learn a new left-hand exercise;
- To learn the notes at the tenth fret.

So far you've learnt two left-hand exercises that should be helping you to develop all of the fingers of your left hand. Today we're going to look at another exercise, one that will last longer than the other two and will give your fingers even more of a workout. This exercise is similar to the one we learnt on Day 5, but with this one I'm going to introduce a new rule: when you run out of strings, move up a fret and go the other way. This may not make sense now, but it will as soon as you begin to play through the exercise!

Exercise 15

As you should see, the first four bars are that same as Exercise 7 from Day 5. Now, instead of reversing what you've just played, move the left hand up one fret and then descend. When you run out of strings again, move up a fret and ascend. This pattern continues all the way up the fretboard (although I haven't written out the complete exercise here).

This is a slightly tougher left-hand exercise than the previous two, but is certainly worth the effort. As with the other exercises, be sure to include this one in your daily warm-up routine.

NOTEBUSTER: THE TENTH FRET

Today we're also going to learn the notes at the tenth fret. These are another relatively easy set, since they're all natural. As you can see from the illustration opposite, the notes we have are D, G, C and F. Remember these notes and, as before, have someone test you on them.

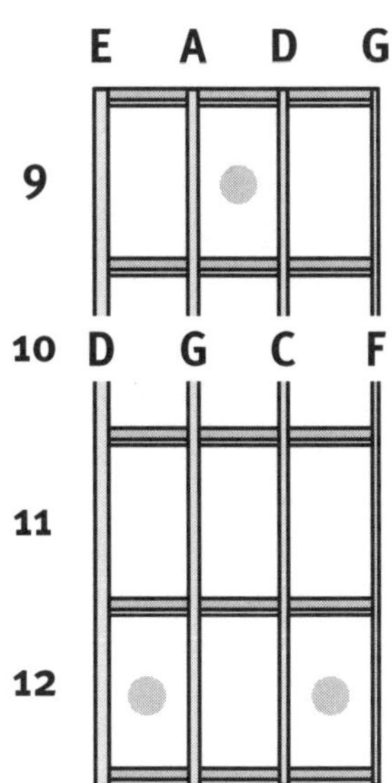

The tenth fret

PRACTICAL EXERCISE

Here is a new bassline for you to study.

Exercise 16

DAY 11 STUDY

1. Add the new left-hand exercise to your warm-up routine.
2. Memorise the notes found at the tenth fret and have someone test you on them.
3. Work on today's Practical Exercise.

DAY 12: THE COMPLETE STAVE

Your goals for Day 12 are:

- To learn the rest of the notes on the stave;
- To learn the notes found at the first fret;
- To learn two new simple basslines.

Today we are going to look again at the bass clef and attempt to fill in some of the blanks. Today you'll learn another seven notes, and you'll need to remember their locations and practise writing them out on the stave. The following stave shows the locations of all the notes available on the stave, up as far as middle C. I've circled the notes you've already learnt, so we're now just filling in the gaps. Remember that the notes you already know will help you to find the others.

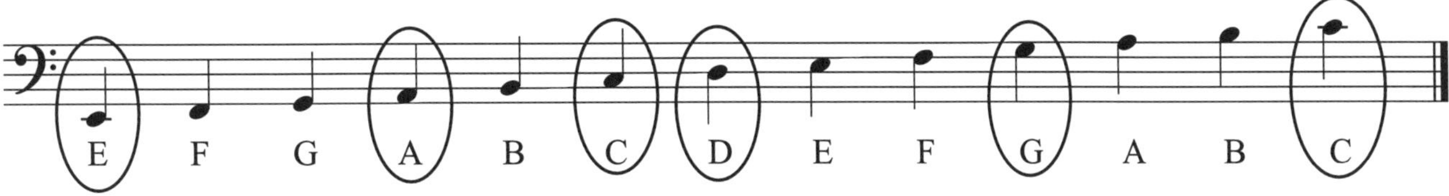

I would suggest learning a note at a time, and writing notes out on a stave will help significantly. There are some empty manuscript pages at the back of the book for you to use.

Bass

NOTEBUSTER: THE FIRST FRET

Today we're going to look at yet another group of notes, this time the ones found at the first fret. As you can see from the illustration, these are F, A♯/B♭, D♯/E♭ and G♯/A♭. You won't fail to notice that we now have a few more sharps and flats to deal with!

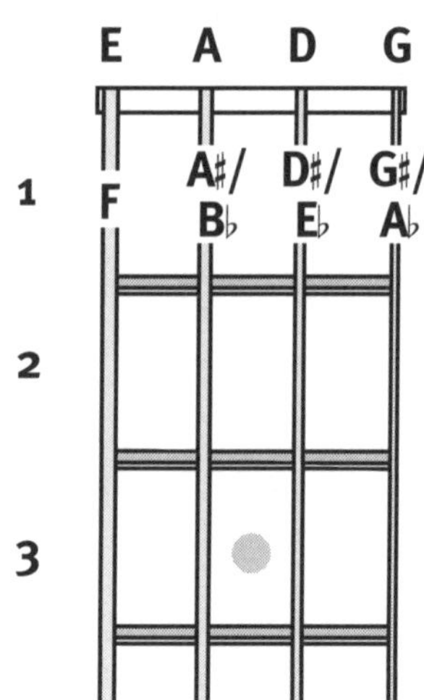

First fret notes

Notice that the first-fret notes for the A, D and G strings are the same notes as the open strings, just sharpened. This may help you to remember them.

DAY 12 STUDY

PRACTICAL EXERCISE

Your final assignment for today is a little more practical, you'll be pleased to hear. Below I've written out another bassline for you to study. This one is a little more difficult, but with a little perseverance you should be able to master it.

Exercise 17

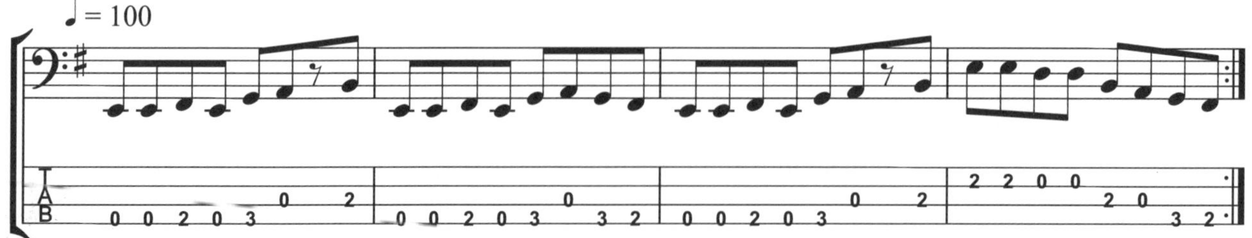

1 On a sheet of manuscript paper, practise writing out the notes we looked at today. You should also try this in a more random order – for example, write out ten different notes, then go back and write their names underneath. Remember, you don't have to master them all today, but be sure to practise them as often as you can.

2 Remember the names of the notes found at the first fret of the bass. Again, have someone test you on these and all the others.

3 Work on today's practical exercises.

DAY 13: THE TRAVELLING THUMB

Your goal for Day 13 is to learn about the travelling-thumb technique.

QUOTE FOR THE DAY

I saw a bass player who was supporting us who used his first and second fingers, but not at once. So I thought I'd use both at once. Later, the same bassist came up to me and said he was influenced by my two finger style and I said, 'Well it came from you!'

– John Entwistle, The Who

Back on Day 4 we began to look at right-hand technique. You'll recall that I showed you how to place your thumb on the pickup to act as an anchor for your fingerstyle playing. This works well, but in playing some of the exercises that use the higher strings, you may have noticed that you're getting excess open string noise. You need to cut all extraneous noise out of your playing from an early stage, so today I'm going to show you how to refine your right-hand technique to do just this.

The technique we are going to look at is known as the *travelling thumb*. Placing your thumb on the pickup works great for playing lines on the E string, but when you play on the other strings, there's a danger of your fingers accidentally touching the E string and allowing it to hum. The solution is to move your thumb so that it rests on the string above the one you are playing. Therefore, if you want to play the A string, for example, move your thumb so that it sits on the E string instead of the pickup. This will prevent it from being able to sound.

This works for the other strings, too. When playing the D, put your thumb on the A string, and when playing the G, put it on the D string. This is what I call the travelling thumb, and you'll hopefully come to think of it as a close friend.

PRACTICAL EXERCISE

Here's an exercise that requires you to use all four strings. Remember to move your thumb anchor every time your move to a new string. You'll see that I have written some thumb guidelines in between the staves. These guides are for these exercises only; they won't usually be there.

Exercise 18

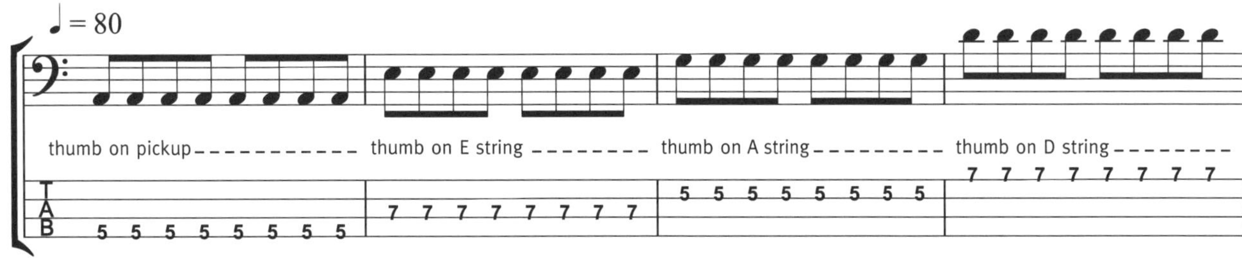

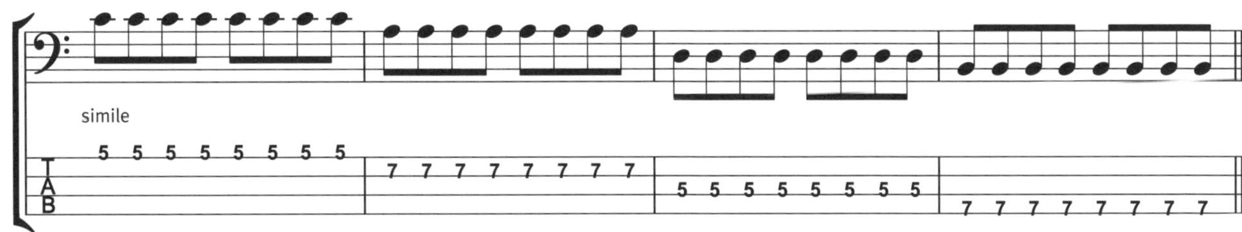

Try to incorporate the travelling-thumb technique into everything you play.

PRACTICAL EXERCISE

To finish off, here's another bassline for you to practise. Be sure to use the travelling-thumb technique!

Exercise 19

I've omitted the guides for this last exercise. See if you can work out the best place for your thumb as you go along.

DAY 13 STUDY

1 Practice the travelling-thumb technique. Try to incorporate it into all areas of your playing, such as warm-ups and all the basslines you've learnt so far.

2 Work on today's Practical Exercises.

3 Practise everything you've learnt this week – tomorrow is test day!

DAY 14

WEEK 2 TEST

Welcome to your second test day. As before, you should complete this test before moving on. Everything you need to know was covered in the last week.

1 Which note is found at the third fret of the A string?

2 Which note is found at the tenth fret of the E string?

3 Which note is found at the first fret of the D string?

4 Which note is found at the tenth fret of the G string?

5 What is an octave?

6 How do you find the octave of any note?

7 Write the note C and its octave on this stave:

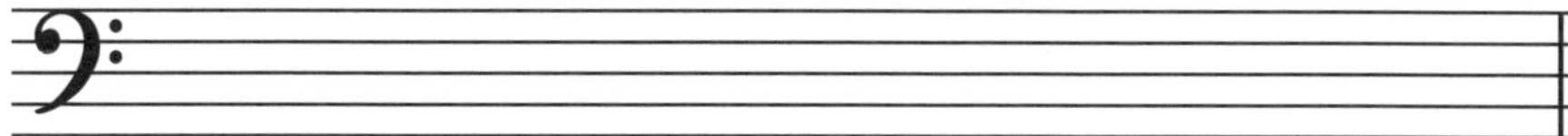

8 How many quarter notes is it possible to have in a bar of 4/4 time?

9 What are the benefits of the travelling-thumb technique?

10 Underneath the stave, write the name of each of these notes:

Exercise 19

TIMED EXERCISE

Finally, here's another new bassline for you to study. Again, you should aim to be able to play this one within 15 minutes.

WEEK 3

OVERVIEW

We now have much of the basic groundwork in place to begin looking at some more practical material. Starting this week, we're going to be looking at *core topics* – different styles of music and some typical basslines from that style. The first style we're going to look at is one of the most common of all: the blues. We'll also continue to develop your music theory and fretboard knowledge. Here's a complete breakdown of what we'll be covering this week:

- **Core Topic: The Blues** – This first core topic covers perhaps the most widely played and accepted style of all.
- **Tuning With Harmonics** – This week we'll look at a more accurate way to tune up, using harmonics.
- **Fretboard Knowledge** – We'll be looking at all of the remaining notes on the fretboard.
- **Left Hand Exercises** – We'll also be learning some new left-hand dexterity exercises that will further develop your fingers.
- **Phrasing Techniques** – Learning phrasing techniques will help you smoothe out your playing; this week, we'll look at the hammer-on and pull-off.
- **Music Notation** – Now that we've looked at quarter notes, we'll be expanding on this and learning how to read and play *eighth notes*.
- **More Basslines** – Of course, we'll be augmenting all of the above with some more practical exercises!

Bass

DAY 15: CORE TOPIC – THE BLUES

Your goals for Day 15 are:

- To learn about the 12-bar blues;
- To learn the notes found at the second fret.

QUOTE FOR THE DAY

Every bass player should be able to play the blues!

– *Stuart Clayton*

It's time to introduce you to one of the most important song structures a musician can learn: the 12-bar blues. The blues dates back to the 19th century and remains a very popular and recognised style to this day. As the name suggests, the 12-bar blues comprises a sequence of 12 bars that is repeated over and over.

The most basic form of the blues, and probably the one that is still most commonly played, has just three chords. Over the page is a blues progression in the key of C, utilising a very simple blues bass part. This sound should be familiar to you – there are literally thousands of songs that use this progression, from 'Johnny B Goode' to 'Jailhouse Rock'. Take a look at the practical exercise over the page.

PRACTICAL EXERCISE

Exercise 20

Study this bass part and become familiar with the sound of it. Make no mistake, one day you will be called upon to play a blues in C, and this is the kind of line you'll need to play. For now, I recommend you learn this line as well as you can. At the end of the week we'll have a look at some alternative bass parts and also a couple of other popular keys for the blues.

Bass

When learning a new style of music, it's very important to listen to as much of it as you can, and to this end Day 20 will include a list of recommended recordings which will help you to develop a better understanding of what you're learning.

NOTEBUSTER: THE SECOND FRET

Today we'll also be studying a new group of notes on the fretboard. We're really just filling in the blanks now, so you can expect a combination of natural notes and sharpened/flattened notes from the remaining frets. Today we will look at the second fret. Once again, here we have a combination of natural notes and sharpened/flattened notes: F♯/G♭, B, E, and A.

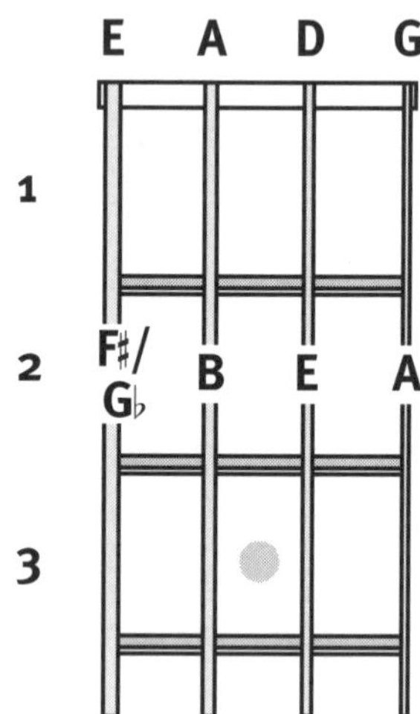

Second fret notes

DAY 15 STUDY

1 Practise the blues in C exercise from this week.

2 Listen to some blues!

3 Memorise the notes at the second fret and have someone test you on these and all the others you've learnt so far.

Bass

DAY 16: EIGHTH NOTES

Your goals for Day 16 are:

- To learn and understand how eighth notes are written and how they sound;
- To learn some eighth-note-based basslines;
- To learn the notes at the fourth fret.

Back on Day 10, we learnt about quarter notes, or crotchets. Today we're going to continue our leisurely look at music notation and look at quavers – or, as they are also, more sensibly known, eighth notes. An eighth note lasts for half the length of a quarter note. (This makes perfect sense if you understand fractions!)

Consequently, we can have two eighth notes on each beat, and a total of eight per bar. This would be counted as *one*-and-*two*-and-*three*-and-*four*-and. You'll see that I've written this under today's exercises to illustrate this more clearly.

You've played some eighth-note passages already in this book – the travelling-thumb exercises from Day 13 were comprised almost entirely of eighth notes, as were many of the exercises from the first week. To further those exercises, here I've written three more bass parts that are based on eighth notes and eighth-note rests. The last exercise also makes use of quarter notes as well as eighth notes. Try to study the notation and understand the rhythms that you see written here. If in doubt, listen to the CD, as always!

Bass

This first exercise is a relentless eighth-note groove. This kind of line would be perfect in a rock setting. You'll see more lines like this one in Week 6, when we'll be taking a closer look at rock music.

Exercise 21

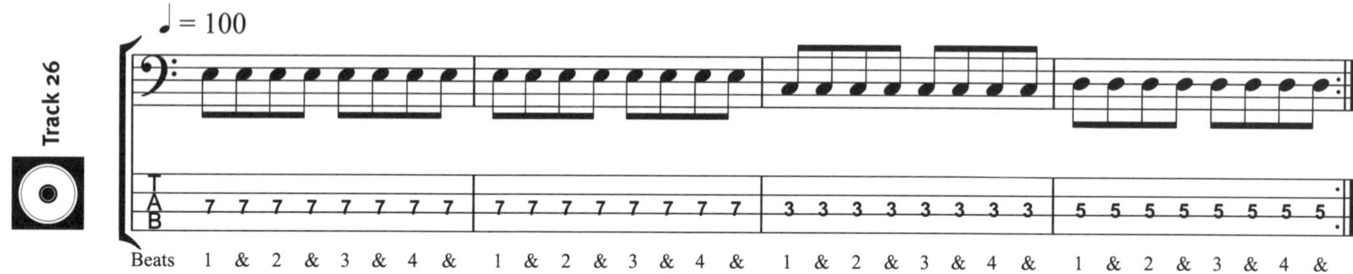

In this next exercise you'll see that I've introduced some eighth-note rests. Note how groups of notes are *beamed* together to make them easier to read:

Exercise 22

This next line also has a continuous eighth-note pulse, but it's broken up by the use of octaves:

Exercise 23

In this next line, the quarter note and its rest are used as well:

Exercise 24

NOTEBUSTER: THE FOURTH FRET

Finally for today, let's take a look at the notes found at the fourth fret. These are G♯/A♭, C♯/D♭, F♯/G♭ and B. You can think of all of these notes (apart from the B) as flattened versions of the notes at the fifth fret.

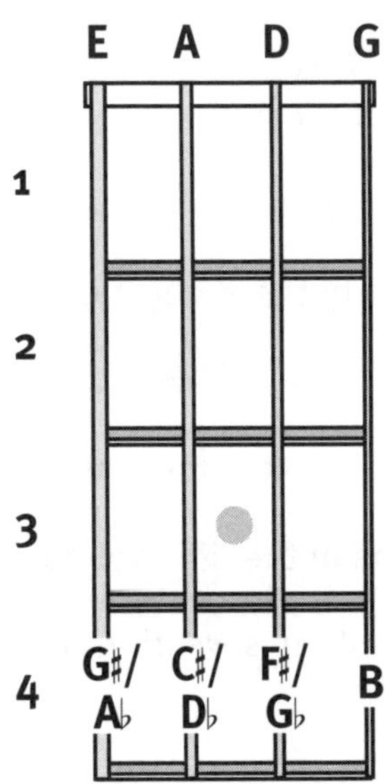

Fourth fret notes

DAY 16 STUDY

1 Practise all of the eighth-note grooves covered today.

2 Look through any music books that you may have (including this one) and see if you can spot any eighth notes and their rests. Try to work out how they might sound.

3 Memorise the sounds of the notes at the fourth fret.

DAY 17: FURTHER LEFT HAND DEVELOPMENT

Your goals for Day 17 are:

- To learn the notes at the sixth fret;
- To learn two new left-hand exercises and understand how to create your own new exercises;
- To learn how to mute notes with the left hand.

NOTEBUSTER: THE SIXTH FRET

Time now to look at the notes at the sixth fret. All of these notes are going to be sharps/flats, also known as *accidentals*. The notes in question are: A♯/B♭, D♯/E♭, G♯/A♭ and C♯/D♭. If it makes them easier to remember, you can think of them either as sharpened versions of the fifth-fret notes or flattened versions of the seventh-fret notes.

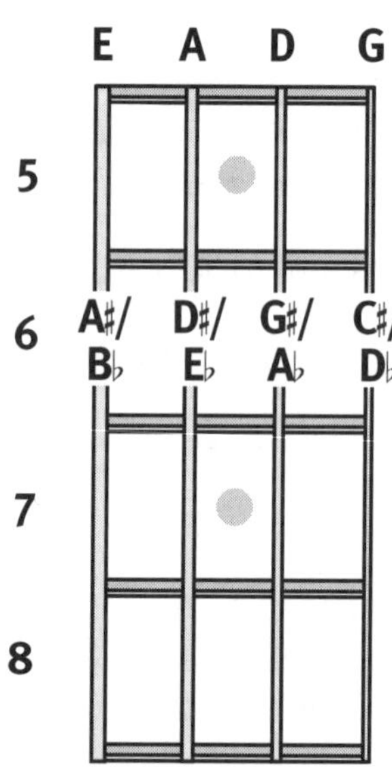

Sixth fret notes

FURTHER LEFT HAND EXERCISES

We've now looked at several chromatic left-hand exercises. If you've been practising them every day, you should find that your left-hand fingers are getting used to playing these patterns and are getting stronger and more dexterous. Today we are going to take our final look at left-hand exercises. This doesn't mean that you should stop practising them, though – far from it! Instead, rather than showing you more and more new exercises, I'm going to explain how you can create your own variations.

So far, you've played only two basic finger patterns: 1, 2, 3, 4 and 4, 3, 2, 1. Many bass parts will require you to play in different sequences, so here we'll be looking at different fingering patterns in order to develop your fingers even further. This exercise will encourage your weaker fingers to work harder and will break you away from the sequences we have played so far.

Our new sequence is going to be 3, 4, 2, 1. Leading with the third finger is tricky and will very likely feel quite uncomfortable, since your fingers will be unused to it. However, this raises a good point: If you can't do something, or are struggling with it, it's generally worth persevering, because the chances are that one day you'll need to do it. Take this exercise at the specified tempo and, as always, try to maintain an even volume and accurate fingering.

Exercise 25

As you can probably see, it's quite easy to come up with several variations using the finger-per-fret approach. Try to come up with some alternatives of your own.

Bass

Remember that exercises like this should form an integral part of your warm-up routine.

LEFT HAND MUTING

Today we're also going to be looking at how to mute notes with the left hand. So far we've allowed each note to ring for its full length, but what if we want short, crisp notes? There are a few ways to achieve them, but the best way is to use the left hand. By lifting the left-hand finger off a fretted note just slightly, you can stop the note ringing. This is quite a simple trick to perform, and a very useful one to have under your belt. The following exercise requires you to play a fairly static bassline but alternate between short and long notes. Short notes have a small dot above them in the notation, representing a dynamic indication known as a *staccato* mark. (We'll be looking more at dynamics in the last week of this course.)

15

Exercise 26

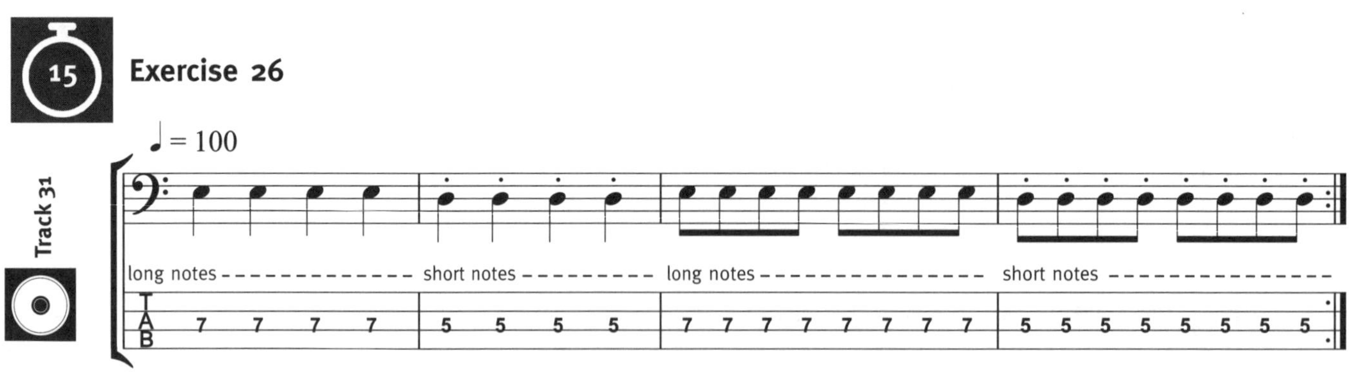

As you'll hear on the CD, there's quite a difference between the long and short notes. This technique of playing staccato is very useful in many styles of music, as you'll discover in some of the later weeks.

DAY 17 STUDY

1 Work these new exercises into your practice regime.

2 Come up with two new left-hand exercises using the information in this section.

3 Memorise the notes found at the sixth fret.

DAY 18: TUNING UP WITH HARMONICS

Your goals for Day 18 are:

- To learn about harmonics and how to tune your bass with them;
- To learn the notes at the eighth fret.

QUOTE FOR THE DAY

People are less capable of manipulating their instrument of choice than they have ever been. A tuner has replaced their ear.

– *Jeff Berlin*

We looked at tuning the bass back on Day 2, and hopefully you've been practising the relative tuning method I showed you then. Today you'll be learning a new way to tune up, one that's slightly more accurate, for reasons that will soon become clear. This new tuning method uses a different kind of note known as an *harmonic*.

HARMONICS

Harmonics are bell-like tones that sound above the bass's usual register. To produce a harmonic, you simply place your finger directly over the actual fret itself without pushing it down. Your finger should be just resting on the string. See the picture of me below playing the harmonic found on the G string at the seventh fret.

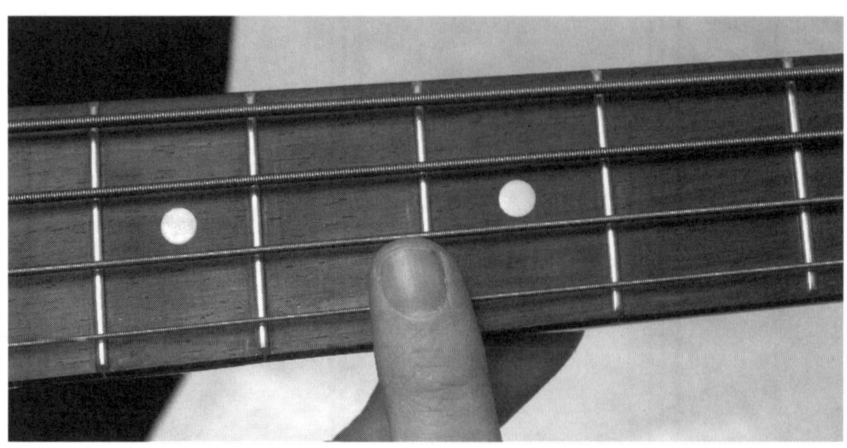

Track 32

When you pluck the string, you should hear a clear, bell-like tone that sounds quite unlike the notes usually produced by the bass.

You may notice that harmonics continue to ring after you've removed your finger from the string. This is useful when it comes to tuning, since it frees up your left hand to adjust the tuning pegs accordingly.

To tune up with harmonics, you first need your G string to be in tune. As before, you need to be sure that you're tuning to something that's already in tune, and for this purpose there's a G reference pitch on Track 32 of the CD.

Once the G is in tune, play the harmonic at the seventh fret of the G string, followed by the harmonic at the fifth fret on the D string. Try to let both ring together, and remember that you can remove your finger from the string after you've played the note. The two notes should be identical, but if they're not, you'll hear a pulse – a rhythmic beating – within the notes that will get slower and disappear as the strings become closer to being in tune. You can hear me bringing two out-of-tune harmonics into tune on (Track 32 of) the CD.

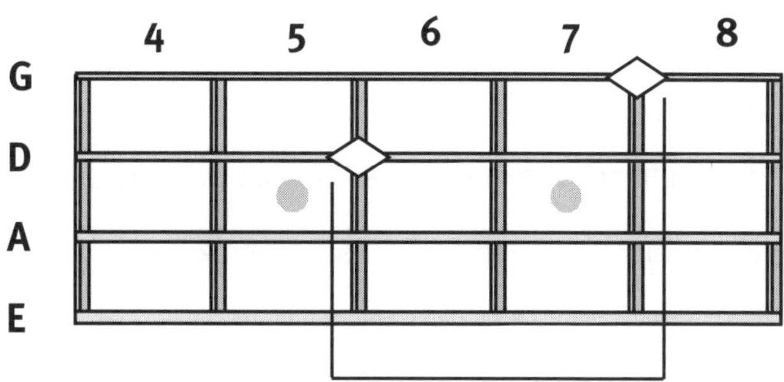

Bass

Once you have these harmonics sounding the same, you can move on to the next pair. Play the seventh fret of the D string and the fifth-fret A-string harmonics together and adjust them accordingly:

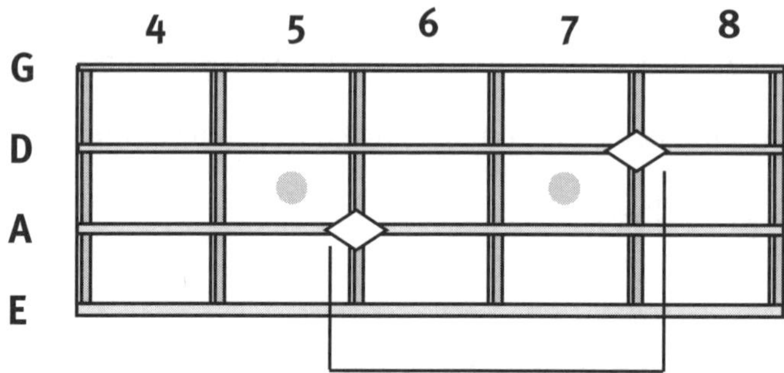

Finally, tune the seventh-fret A-string and fifth-fret E-string harmonics together:

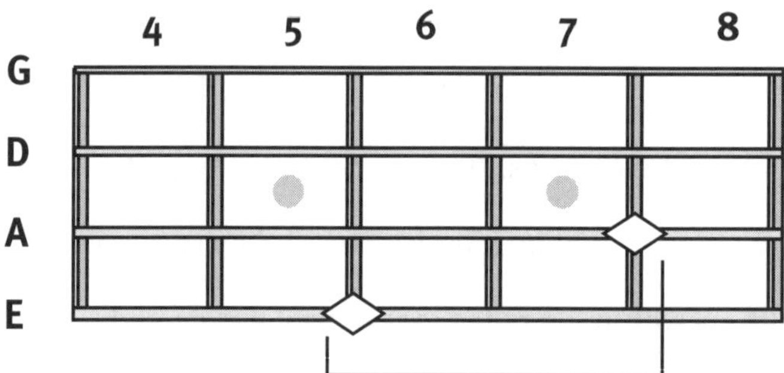

Your bass should now be in tune.

As with the first method of tuning, you'll need to make sure that you get each pair of strings as accurately in tune as possible, as even small discrepancies will result in an out-of-tune instrument.

Bass

NOTEBUSTER: THE EIGHTH FRET

Today we'll also be looking at the notes found at the eighth fret. You'll be pleased to hear that this time there are a couple of natural notes! The four notes are: C, F, A♯/B♭ and D♯/E♭.

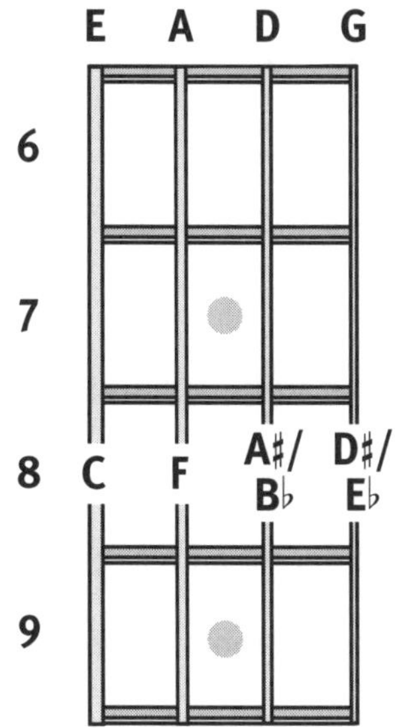

Eighth fret notes

PRACTICAL EXERCISE

Finally for today, a simple bassline for you to work on.

Exercise 27

DAY 18 STUDY

1 Practise tuning your bass using harmonics.

2 Add the notes at the eighth fret to your repertoire.

3 Practise today's exercise.

DAY 19: PHRASING TECHNIQUES

Your goals for Day 19 are:

- To learn about the two most basic phrasing techniques: the hammer-on and the pull-off;
- To learn the notes at the 11th fret.

There are several different phrasing techniques available to you as a bassist. Phrasing techniques are tools that enable you to play with more feeling and fluidity, and all players use them differently. These tools will help you to find your own sound on the bass and will help you considerably in finding your own voice on the instrument.

We'll look at all of the many phrasing techniques available to you throughout the course of this book, but today we're going to concentrate on the two most basic tools: the hammer-on and the pull-off. You may well have heard of these strange-sounding customers before, especially if you have guitar-playing friends. But what are they? Let's find out...

SLURS

Hammer-ons and pull-offs are both what we call *slurs*. A slur is simply a way of playing two or more notes smoothly after plucking the string just once. Rest assured, you'll understand these terms better once you've put them into practice!

THE HAMMER-ON

In the first example below, which you can also hear on Track 34 of the CD, I've written out a simple hammer-on. To play it, fret the D at the fifth fret of the A string with your first finger. Play the note, and then bring the third or fourth finger of your left hand down onto the E at the seventh fret. As the string is still moving, the note will sound and you should have a nice, smooth transition from the D to the E.

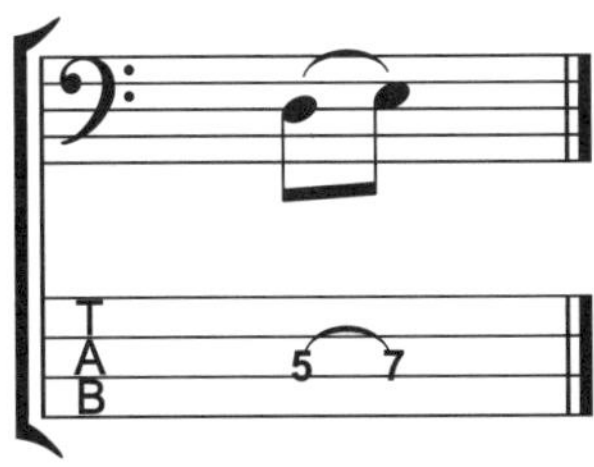

Hammer-on

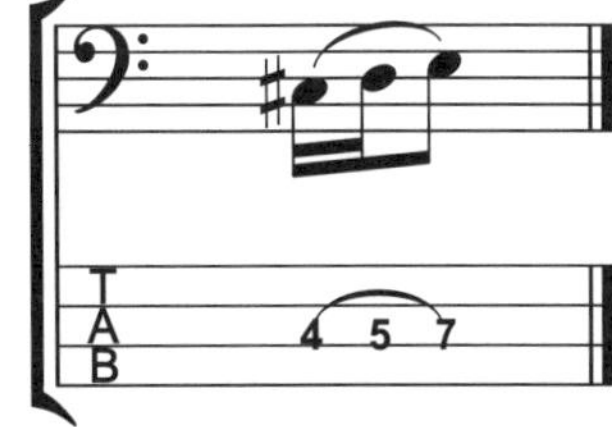

Multiple hammer-on

You'll need to hammer onto the E with a little force in order for the two notes to sound at the same volume. Listen to the CD and aim for the sound you hear there. With a little practice, you should learn how much force you need to use. Since you have four available fingers on your left hand, multiple hammer-ons are also possible. The second example shows a C♯ being played, followed by a hammer-on to the D with the second finger and then the E with the fourth finger. You can hear me playing this on the CD.

THE PULL-OFF

The pull-off is the mirror opposite of the hammer-on. In the first example below, the E at the seventh fret is played first, while the finger fretting the E then lifts up, allowing the fretted D at the fifth fret to sound. Obviously, you need to have your first finger in position at the D before you pull-off.

Pull-off

Multiple pull-off

Again, refer to the CD and try to emulate what you hear. Both notes should be similar in volume, just as they were for the hammer-on. Multiple pull-offs are also possible, although these really are guitar players' favourites, so don't overuse them! When trying out the second example above, play the E as before, then pull off to the D (which is already fretted by the second finger), then pull off to the C♯ (fretted by the first finger). Again, you can hear me playing these on Track 34 of the CD.

Notice that hammer-ons and pull-offs always have a curved line over them to indicate that they're slurred.

NOTEBUSTER: THE ELEVENTH FRET

You'll be pleased to know that this is last group of notes we need to look at, and comprises D♯/E♭, G♯/A♭, C♯/D♭ and F♯/G♭. Now all you need to do is remember them all! Next week we'll be looking at ways to do just that.

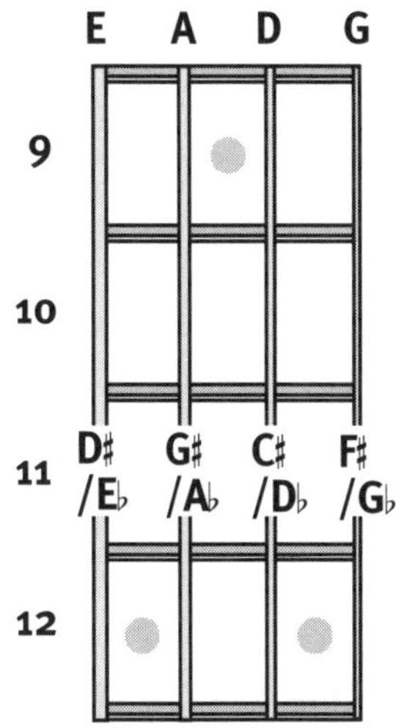

PRACTICAL EXERCISE

I leave you today with a new bassline that makes use of hammer-ons and pull-offs. Work with the CD to get this right, and try to incorporate these phrasing tools into your playing from this point on.

30 **Exercise 28**

DAY 19 STUDY

1 What does the musical term 'slur' mean?

2 Practise the phrasing tools and bassline introduced this week.

Bass

DAY 20: CORE TOPIC – BLUES BASSLINES

Your goals for Day 20 are:

- To learn the notes at the 11th fret;
- To further your knowledge of the blues by learning two new blues basslines.

At the beginning of this week, we looked at the basic 12-bar blues pattern. Hopefully you'll have been practising the pattern I gave you and are now ready to tackle another. In today's lesson, we're going to look at two new 12-bar blues patterns: the first is in the key of C (which you will already be familiar with) and the second in the key of E (another very popular key for the blues). You should learn these lines as well as you can, and eventually, when your playing has progressed to the appropriate standard, learn them in other keys as well. The blues is one of the simplest song forms and is played in many different keys.

PRACTICAL EXERCISE

The following exercise has a rocky feel. You should be familiar with this type of feel, having studied eighth-note grooves earlier this week. Notice how the bassline 'walks' up from one chord to another – for example, check out the ascending line in bar 4. Lines such as this one help to push the line along and give it a sense of movement. Pay attention to the left-hand fingering shown here.

Exercise 29

Track 36

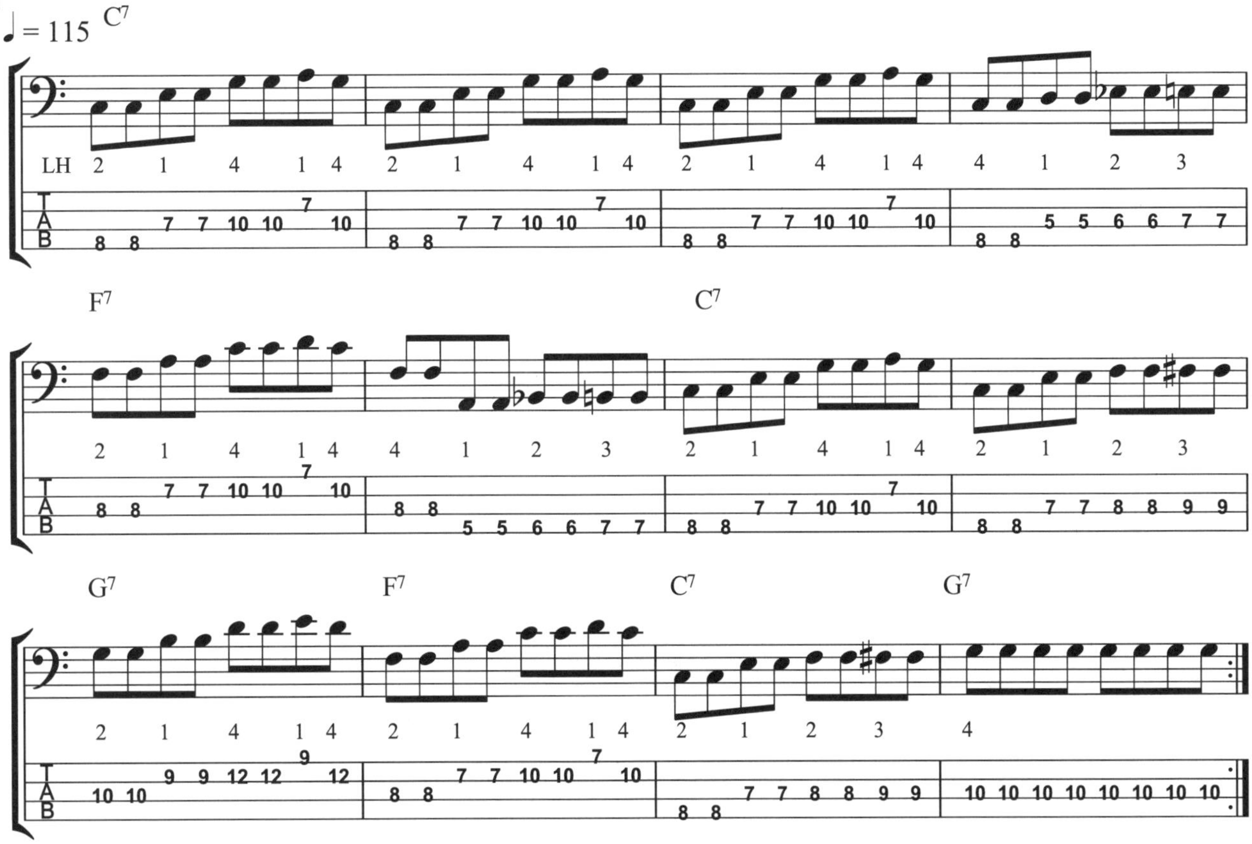

♩ = 115 C7

LH

F7 C7

G7 F7 C7 G7

PRACTICAL EXERCISE

The second exercise is a blues in E and has what's known as a *shuffle feel*. (You'll see what I mean when you hear Track 37 on the CD.) This is another popular device in the blues. Note the mixture of quarter notes and eighth notes, allowing the line to move along where necessary and relax where necessary. You'll also notice the use of those 'walking' lines discussed earlier.

Bass

Exercise 30

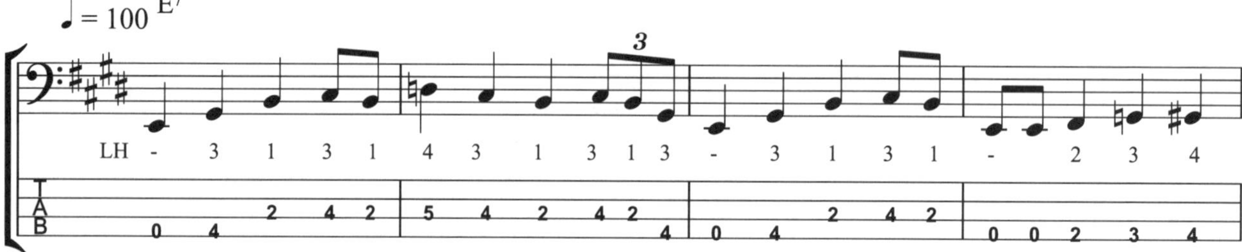

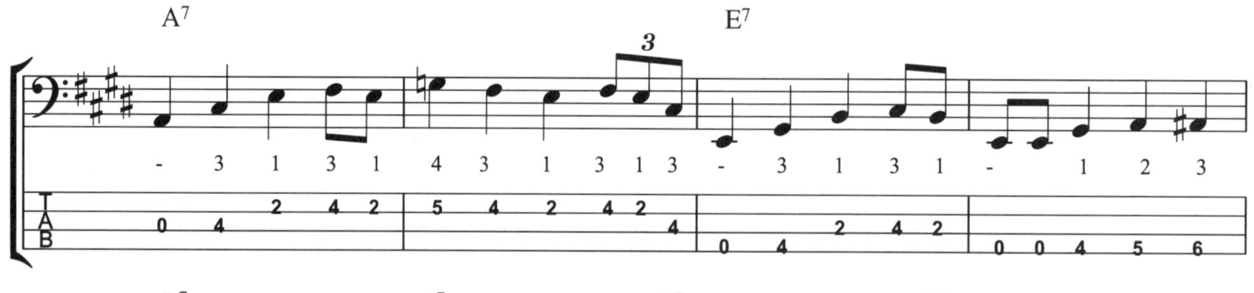

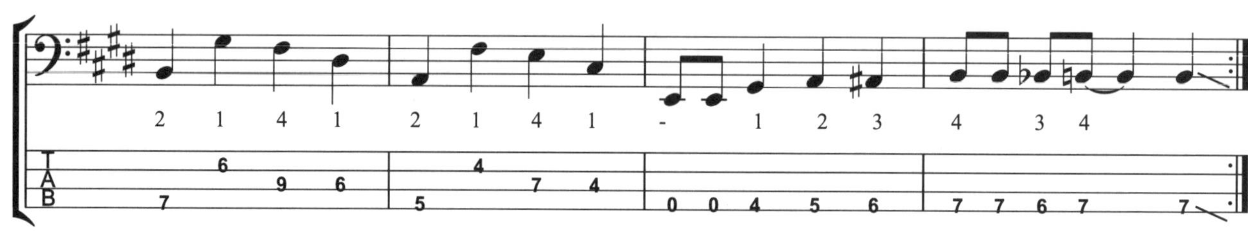

There's quite a lot of material in each of these lines, so take them slowly, and be sure to keep an eye on the left-hand fingerings I have annotated between staves.

The Blues Brothers: 'Sweet Home Chicago'

Elvis Presley: 'Jailhouse Rock'

Chuck Berry: 'Johnny B Goode'

Chuck Berry: 'No Particular Place To Go'

Muddy Waters: 'Hoochie Coochie Man'

Elvis Presley: 'Blue Suede Shoes'

The Commitments: 'Mustang Sally'

Jimi Hendrix: 'Red House'

John Lee Hooker: 'Walkin' The Dog'

Gary Moore: 'Still Got The Blues'

DAY 20 STUDY

1 Work on the blues basslines presented in this chapter.

2 Make sure you're familiar with everything we have covered this week. Tomorrow is another big test day!

Bass

DAY 21

WEEK 3 TEST

Today is your third test day. As before, you should complete this test before moving on. Everything you need to know was covered in the last week.

---

1 How many chords are there in a basic blues progression?

2 Which note is found at the second fret of the E string?

3 How many eighth notes is it possible to have in a bar of 4/4 time?

4 Which note is found at the fourth fret of the A string?

5 What does *staccato* mean?

6 What are the benefits of tuning with harmonics?

7 Which note is found at the eighth fret of the G string?

8 What is a slur?

9 What is a hammer-on?

10 What is a pull-off?

TIMED EXERCISE

Finally, here's another new bassline for you to study. This is another 12-bar blues, this time in the key of A. Note the addition of a D7 chord in the second bar. You should aim to be able to play this one within about 30 minutes.

30

Track 38

♩ = 100 A7 D7 A7

D7 A7

E7 D7 A7 E7

WEEK 4

OVERVIEW

Now that we've begun to look at musical styles, I'm hoping that many of the concepts covered in previous weeks are beginning to make some sense. This week, we'll be following on from our look at the blues and examining another well-known style: pop music. In addition to this, you'll be furthering your knowledge of the fretboard and music notation and finding out about scales. Here's a full breakdown of what will be covered:

- **Core Topic: Pop Music** – A new chapter, a new style. This week we'll look at pop music and learn four typical pop basslines.

- **The Major Scale** – Everyone has heard of scales and no doubt thinks it's best to avoid them! This week I'll be attempting to demystify the major scale.

- **Fretboard Knowledge** – Now that you've studied the notes at each fret, this week it's time to look at some new approaches that will help you get those notes off the fretboard and into your head!

- **Music Notation** – Following our look at quarter notes and eighth notes, this week we'll be slowing things down a little and taking a peek at half notes and whole notes.

- **Phrasing Techniques** – A new phrasing technique to play with this week: the slide.

Bass

DAY 22: CORE TOPIC – POP MUSIC

Your goal for Day 22 is to learn about pop music and play some typical pop basslines.

QUOTE FOR THE DAY

Bands can play anything if they're good, it doesn't matter what kind of music it is, it's just got to be good.

– Norman Watt-Roy, The Blockheads

The term *pop music* is fairly broad and covers a lot of music. As a bass player, it's one of the styles of music that you will be called upon to play again and again. Pop took off in the late '50s with the advent of rock 'n' roll, a style that created the first musical superstars. It was a time when LPs became readily available and young people began to buy them in much larger quantities than any previous format. This created a mass market that spawned many musical heroes and made household names of artists such as The Beatles and The Beach Boys.

Pop music is characterised by relatively straightforward chord progressions, catchy melodies (*hooks*) and memorable riffs (short melodic or rhythmic fragments repeated throughout a song – for example, the intro riff to Roy Orbison's 'Pretty Woman').

Today we'll be looking at three pop basslines. Each is based on a common chord progression found in pop music.

PRACTICAL EXERCISE

You'll need to use open strings in this exercise. This line is made up of continuous eighth notes, but notice that the middle two of every bar are tied together, making things slightly easier. (Ties are covered in Week 5, if you need to skip ahead.)

Bass

Exercise 31

PRACTICAL EXERCISE

This eighth-note-based exercise also makes use of arpeggios.

Exercise 32

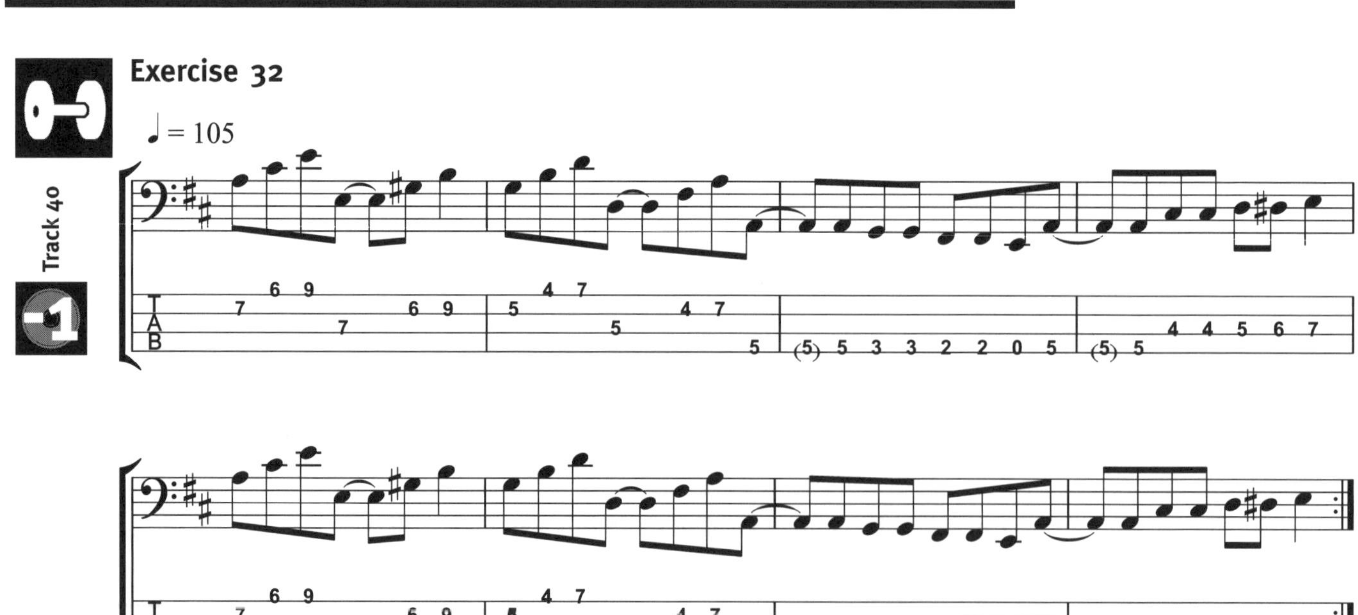

DAY 22 STUDY

1 Learn the two pop basslines introduced in this section.

2 What is a riff?

DAY 23: THE MAJOR SCALE

Your goal for Day 23 is to learn how to play the major scale.

Scales are an important and much misunderstood aspect of music. While there are certainly more interesting things to be playing, scales are nonetheless vital for helping you grow as a musician. If studied correctly, they will help you to understand your instrument better. There are two types of scale that we will cover in this book, major and minor, and while we won't be studying them in too much depth, I believe it's good for you to be introduced to them during the early days of your playing. In total, there are 12 major scales and 12 minor scales, and we'll be covering them all in this book – but don't panic! It's easier than it sounds.

The major scale should sound familiar to you. Below is a C major scale for you to practise; play through it, being careful to abide by the left-hand fingering provided. You can also hear it played on Track 41 of the CD.

Over the page is a fretboard representation of the scale. The black dots represent the root (C) and its octave:

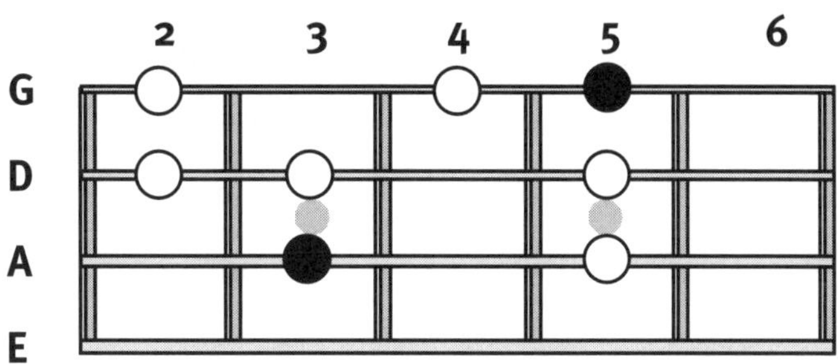

This fretboard pattern is completely moveable. You could move the entire pattern to any other note on the bass and it would have the same sound, although it would obviously be a different scale. Go ahead and try this – move the pattern up two frets so that you start on D. You'll then have this:

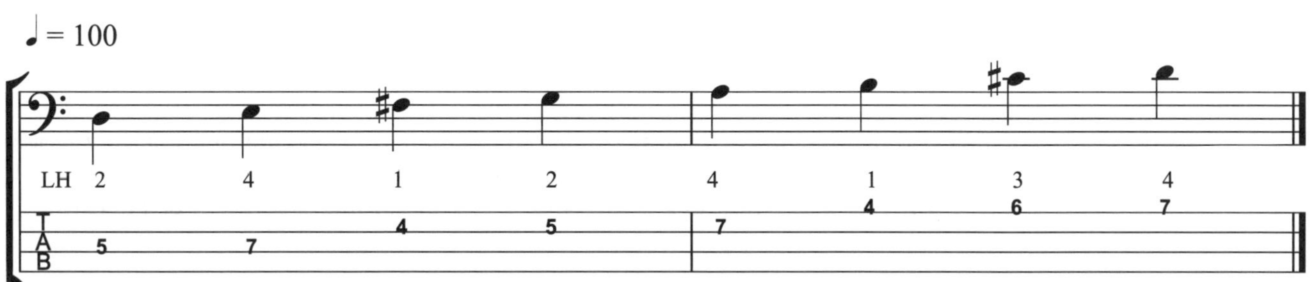

You've just played a D major scale!

Bass

INTERVALS

Moving scales *en masse* in this way is possible because the major scale is created from a specific set of *intervals* (the distance between two notes). Major and minor scales contains two intervals: the tone and the semitone. A tone is the distance from one note to another note two frets away (the distance from C to D, for example), while a semitone is the distance from a note to the note one fret away (the distance between E and F, for example), as shown below:

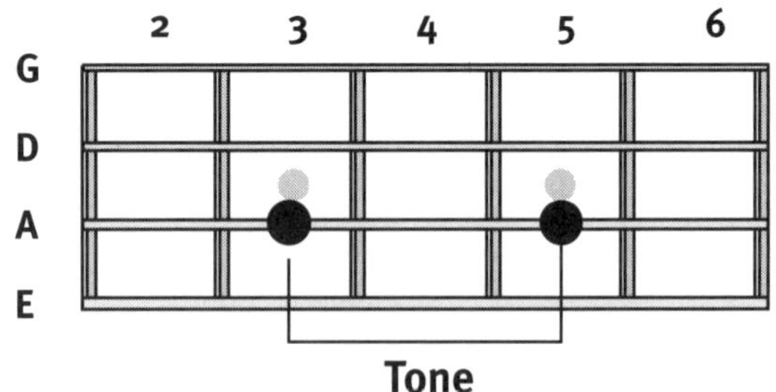

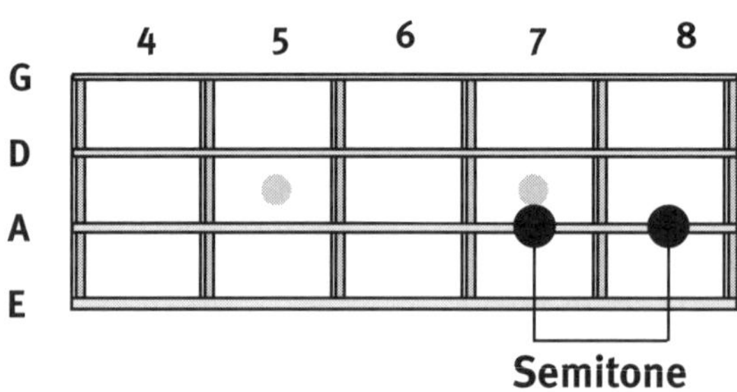

As you can see in the diagram below, the C major scale is made up of the following set of intervals: tone, tone, semitone, tone, tone, tone, semitone, or TTSTTTS.

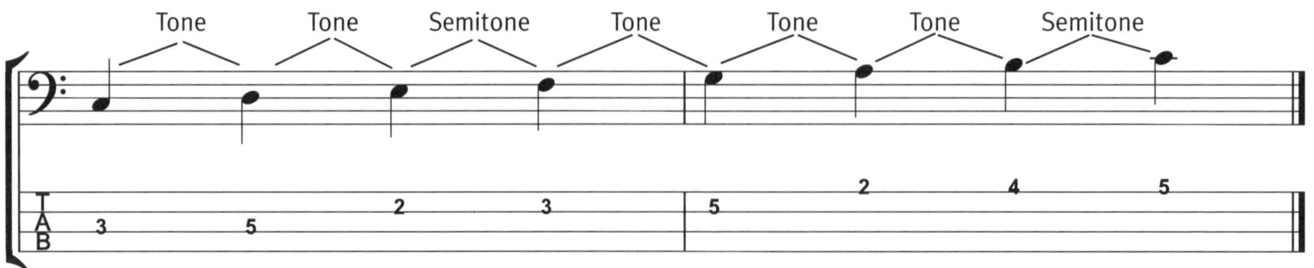

This pattern of intervals is what defines a major scale.

Today I've introduced quite a few new terms and concepts, and I suggest that you take your time to digest the information presented here. Using the information you've learned today, you should be able to play a major scale in any key.

DAY 23 STUDY

1 What is an interval?

2 What is the interval distance between C and D?

3 What is the interval distance between E and F?

4 Can you play an E major scale? (Everything you need to know in order to do this is in today's lesson!)

DAY 24: A FINAL LOOK AT THE FRETBOARD

Your goal for Day 24 is to learn some new ways to become familiar with the notes on the fretboard.

QUOTE FOR THE DAY

The majority of musicians can't read music, can't play in different keys on their instruments, don't know the names of certain sounds and chords and don't know the notes on their guitars. It's not an insult; it's a fact. – *Jeff Berlin*

Over the past three weeks I've gradually introduced you to all the of the notes on the fretboard of your bass. Hopefully by now you'll know a few of them, or at least be able to work them out. Today we're going to look at some exercises that will enable you to practise them. As I told you back on Day 6, it's very important to know the fretboard as well as you can, as this will make it easier to tackle many other aspects of your playing, such as scales. Be sure to add one or more of these exercises to your daily practice routine. You don't need to do them all every day (unless you want to!), but you should aim to cover them all over the duration of the eight weeks of this course.

With all of the following methods, you should say the name of each note aloud as you play it.

METHOD 1

This is the simplest method and a good place to start. Take a look at the diagram at the top of the next page. Begin on the E string and work your way along chromatically (ie a note at a time), naming the notes as you play them:

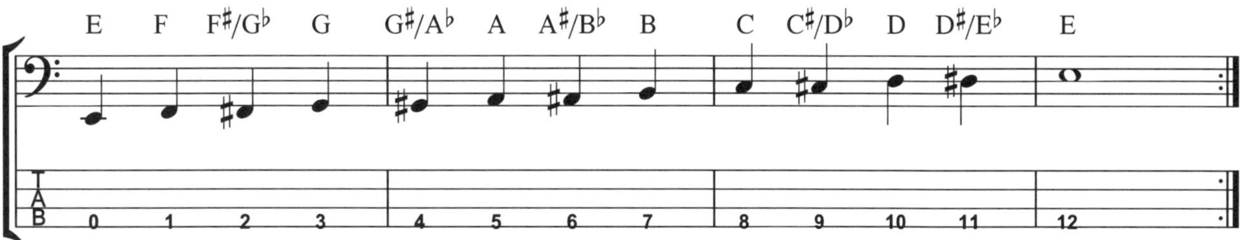

This method might be a good place to start, but it has a disadvantage in that it tends to encourage you to learn the notes parrot-fashion. For example, if someone pointed to a random note and asked you to name it, you might find that you need to count along the string in order to find that note's name. You might argue that you got there in the end, but the truth is that your fretboard knowledge will need to be much quicker and more independent. The next two methods should help you to break from the parrot-fashion style of learning.

METHOD 2

This method breaks away from the chromatic approach. Here, every odd-numbered fret is played ascending and every even numbered fret descending. Take a look at the illustration below:

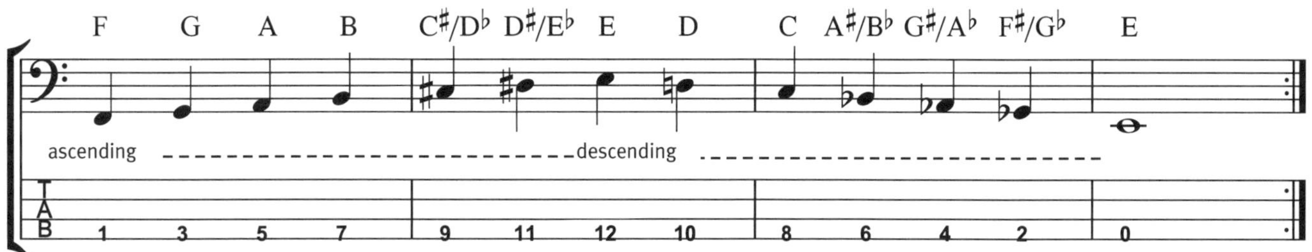

You need to repeat this on each string of your bass.

Bass

METHOD 3

This one is quite tricky and is the ultimate test of your fretboard knowledge! The idea of this exercise is to disassociate your mind from any of the previous patterns. This method uses just the first and second fingers of your left hand, and you'll need to slide up a fret when you run out of strings. It sounds confusing, but a glance at the illustration below should clear things up:

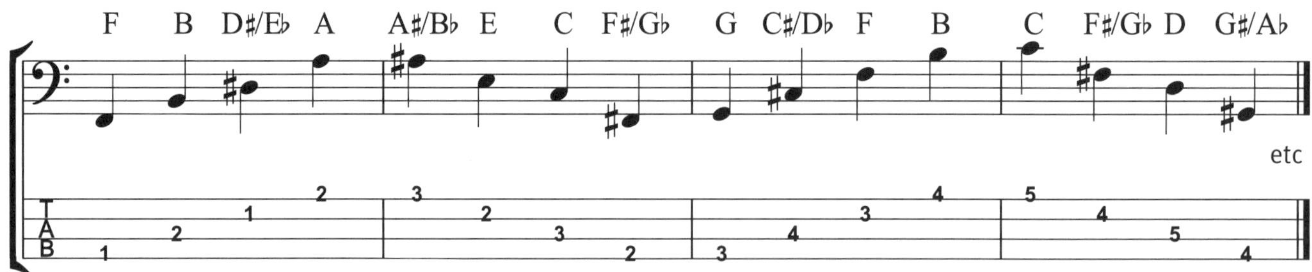

As I mentioned earlier, you should include one of these methods in your daily practice routine.

PRACTICAL EXERCISE

Finally for today, I leave you with another exercise to work on.

Bass

DAY 24 STUDY

1 Practise the fretboard-learning exercises introduced this week.

2 Work on today's practical exercise.

DAY 25: THE SLIDE – A NEW PHRASING TOOL

On Day 19, we began to look at the various phrasing techniques available to bass players, particularly hammer-ons and pull-offs. Hopefully, at this stage you're still practising them and integrating them into your playing. Today we're going to be looking at the other popular techniques that are frequently used by bassists.

QUOTE FOR THE DAY

I'm more interested in talking about how to phrase a melody and create a solo that goes someplace.

– Stu Hamm

SLIDES

As you can hear on Track 43 of the CD, slides are played by literally sliding from one note to the next, and all bassists use them to some degree. They are very simple to play and sound great if used sensibly. Slides can also be used in place of hammer-ons and pull offs and have a slightly different sound. (The technical term for a slide is a *glissando*.)

At the top of the next page are two basslines that incorporate slides. Listen closely to the CD to hear how they should sound:

Exercise 34

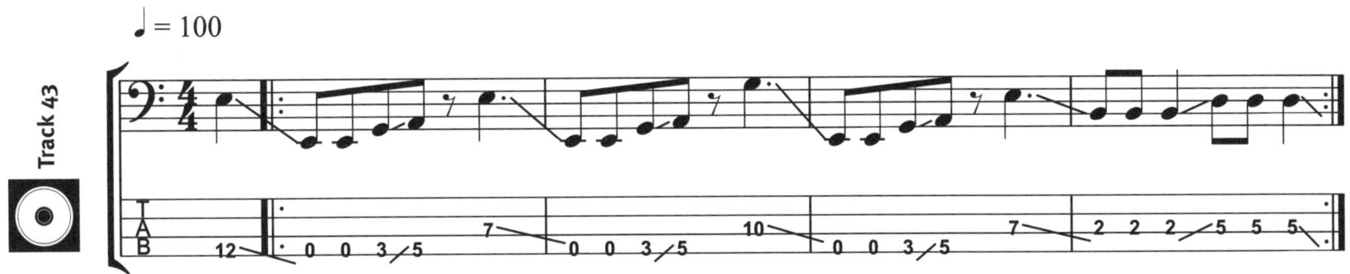

It's very common for a bassist to play a descending slide on the beat before entering at the start of a song or a new section. To play the intro slide, fret the E string at the 12th fret, play it and then slide your finger down the string.

Remember that it's important not to overuse any of these phrasing techniques. They're much more effective if used sparingly.

PRACTICAL EXERCISE

Your second practical exercise for today – shown over the page – is another blues bassline, and in this one I've incorporated some phrasing tools. This one looks a lot harder than it is; the pattern introduced in the first bar is used for the rest of the line, just in different places.

Bass

Exercise 35

DAY 25 STUDY

1 Practise all of the exercises introduced this week and try to incorporate the techniques into your playing.

DAY 26: HALF NOTES AND WHOLE NOTES

Your goal for Day 26 is to understand whole notes and half notes and how to read them.

In previous weeks we've looked at reading quarter notes and eighth notes. It can take a fair bit of practice to get comfortable with reading these rhythms, let alone learn all the notes on the bass clef. With that in mind, you might feel that learning two new rhythms is going to make things even worse. Well, worry not, as the two note values we're going to look at today are pretty slow – slower than either of the values we've looked at so far.

HALF NOTES

If you refer back to the rhythm table on Day 10, you'll see that half notes (or *minims*, as they're known in UK terminology) last for two beats. This means that they're twice as long as quarter notes. Take a look at the bass part shown below, which uses only half notes. It's very simple, and if you listen to the CD you should be able to hear that half notes go by pretty slowly!

Exercise 36

There will be some simple exercises like this for you to study at the end of the day.

WHOLE NOTES

Whole notes are even easier to play than half notes, as they last for a whole bar, as you'll be able to see from Day 10's chart. Have a look at the following bass part, which uses only whole notes and so should be quite straightforward:

Exercise 37

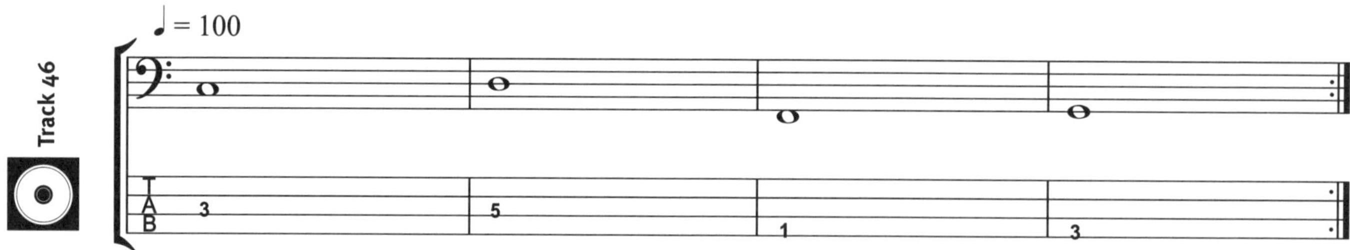

The next bassline has been designed to enable you to study and practise half notes, whole notes and their respective rests. You shouldn't have too much difficulty with this one, as it's quite slow. As always, you should refer to the CD and play along:

Exercise 38

! **Be sure to keep referring back to quarter-note and eighth-note rhythms as well.**

Bass

PRACTICAL EXERCISES

The following lines are made up of all the rhythms we've looked at so far.

Exercise 39

Exercise 40

DAY 26 STUDY

1 Practise all of the exercises introduced this week.

2 Look through some music books to see how whole notes and half notes are used. Try to work out how the music would sound.

Bass

DAY 27: CORE TOPIC – POP BASSLINES

Your goal for Day 27 is to learn two more pop basslines.

Following the introduction to pop music at the beginning of the week, we'll be ending the week with another selection of pop basslines. Again, these are relatively common lines that are extremely good for you to know as a bass player. Some are a little more advanced than those you've played previously, but with a little diligence and hard work you'll be able to achieve the desired results.

QUOTE FOR THE DAY

For me, it's looking to the drummer. I lock in with the drummer. If the drummer is hitting all the right grooves, that gives me all I need.

– Norman Watt-Roy, The Blockheads

Exercise 41

♩ = 105

Bass

Exercise 42

As I said earlier, pop music is a very broad term and one which covers a great deal of music. As with all styles, you will come to understand it better the more you listen to it. Here are a broad selection of tracks that I suggest checking out:

The Beatles: 'Lady Madonna'
Michael Jackson: 'Thriller'
ABBA: 'Dancing Queen'
S Club 7: 'Don't Stop Movin''
REM: 'Losing My Religion'
Bob Dylan: 'Brown Eyed Girl'
M-People: 'Movin' On Up'
Level 42: 'Lessons In Love'
Sixpence None The Richer: 'Kiss Me'
Coldplay: 'Yellow'

DAY 27 STUDY

1 Learn and practise the four pop basslines presented in this section.

2 Look back over everything we've looked at this week. Tomorrow is test day again!

Bass

DAY 28

WEEK 4 TEST

Today is your third test day. As before, you should complete this test before moving on. Everything you need to know was covered in the last week.

1 What is a riff?

2 What's the difference between a tone and a semitone?

3 What's the sequence of tones and semitones that defines a major scale?

4 How many major scales are there?

5 Which note is found at the eighth fret of the D string?

6 What's the other name for a slide?

7 Why are phrasing tools so important?

8 How many half notes is it possible to have in a bar of 4/4?

9 How many whole notes is it possible to have in a bar of 4/4?

10 Which note is found at the ninth fret of the E string?

TIMED EXERCISE

Finally, here's another new pop bassline for you to study. You should aim to be able to play this one within 30 minutes. Look out for use of patterns and repetition.

WEEK 5

OVERVIEW

Following our look at pop music in the previous week, we're now going to look at disco music and some basslines that best represent the style. We'll also look at scales and music notation in some more depth, as well some new phrasing tools. Here's a complete breakdown of what we'll be looking at in the coming week:

- **Core Topic: Disco Music** – This week we'll look at a brief history of this well-known style and learn four disco basslines.

- **Major Scales** – Now that you can play a major scale, it's time to look at how to go about practising all 12 of them.

- **Music Notation** – This week we are going to look at extending the note values already explored with ties and dots.

- **Phrasing Tools** – Three new phrasing tools to spice up your playing this week: the trill, vibrato and string bending.

- **The Minor Scale** – Having covered the major scale last week, this week we're going to look at one of the other important scales, the minor.

DAY 29: CORE TOPIC – DISCO MUSIC

Your goal for Day 29 is to learn about disco music and to play some typical disco basslines.

Disco music began life in American clubs and was popular in the mid 1970s, thanks in no small part to the hit movie *Saturday Night Fever*. The focus of disco was on dancing and having a good time, and this led to tracks being *remixed* to be longer than the average pop song, finally culminating in the arrival of the 12" remix that was so popular throughout the '80s.

QUOTE FOR THE DAY

It's healthy that people listen to lots of different types of stuff. I was watching MTV the other day and it was great to see lots of different stuff going on rather than seeing it all categorised.

– Steve Harris, Iron Maiden

Disco music is characterised by many things. Firstly the tempo is usually in the range of 110–140bpm – a range no doubt dictated by dancing speeds. Secondly, disco lyrics are generally about having a good time, dancing and fashion.

The bass player's role in disco is very important. You must be able to play a danceable groove whatever style of music you're playing, and this is especially crucial with disco. As you'll discover from today's exercises, disco basslines are characterised by pumping eighth-note lines, octaves and slightly more advanced chord sequences. Tempo-wise, all of these exercises are in the region of 100–110bpm, which is perhaps a little slower than they would normally be played. Once you're comfortable with them, you might want to practise them a little quicker with a metronome or drum machine.

As before, you can hear the bass tracks on the CD. The second time through each track, the bass will drop out so that you can practise the line with the backing track.

Bass

This first disco line is built around a continuous eighth-note figure. (We covered eighth notes back on Day 16, so hopefully this line won't pose too many difficulties in that regard.) In the last two bars, you'll notice the use of *octaves* – a very common feature in disco. Also, note the staccato marks above the higher notes; these can shortened using the left-hand muting technique discussed on Day 17.

Exercise 43

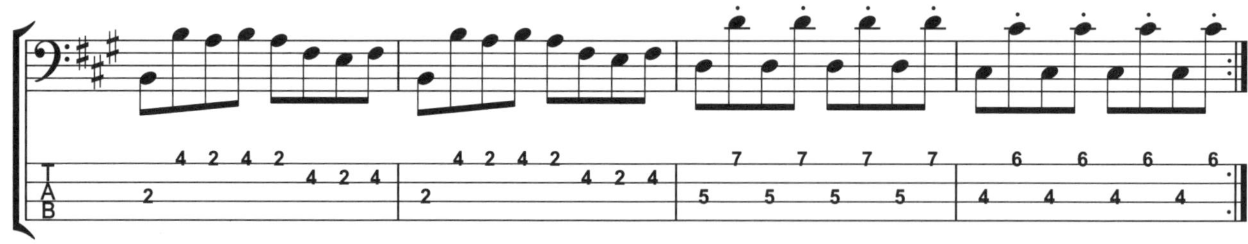

The second exercise for today is again based on an eighth note figure. To play the figure in the first bar (which is then re-used frequently in this line), fret the D with your first finger, the A with your third and the octave D with your fourth. Lines like this can be tricky, since there is so much string crossing involved, but if you start slowly and make sure you understand exactly what you're playing, you shouldn't experience too many difficulties.

Exercise 44

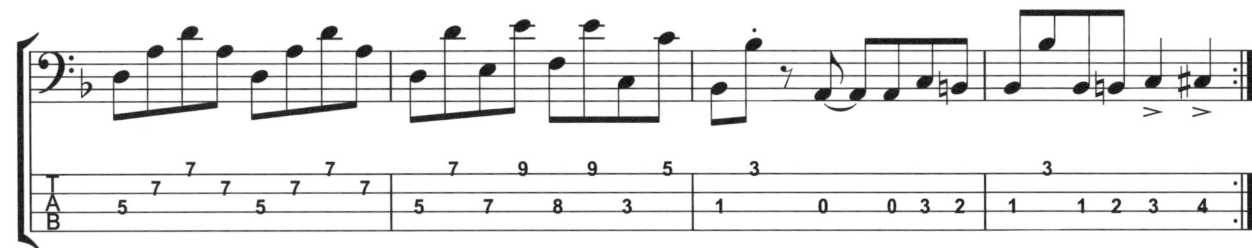

Good luck with these lines. They're quite tricky, and you should feel pretty good once you have them down.

There will be a few more lines like this on Day 34.

DAY 29 STUDY

1 Practise the bass parts introduced this week.

DAY 30: HOW TO PRACTISE SCALES

Your goal for Day 30 is to learn the circle of fifths and how to use it to practise your scales.

QUOTE FOR THE DAY

I encourage people to transcribe the work of other bass players as well as all instruments, and just play along and try to assimilate the music.

– Mark Egan

On Day 23 I showed you how to play a major scale. Not only that, but we looked at the basic theory behind a major scale and discovered that by moving the pattern around it's possible to play a major scale in any key you like. It's good practice to play through all 12 major scales and it also makes for a good warm-up exercise, one that's slightly more interesting than the chromatic exercises we've been using so far.

There is a very logical way to practise your major scales using a sequence known as the *circle of fifths*. This comprises a sequence of all 12 keys arranged in a specific order. You don't need to know too much about the circle of fifths for now, but by learning what it is at this early stage you'll be better equipped to put your scales to use in the future. Here it is in all its glory:

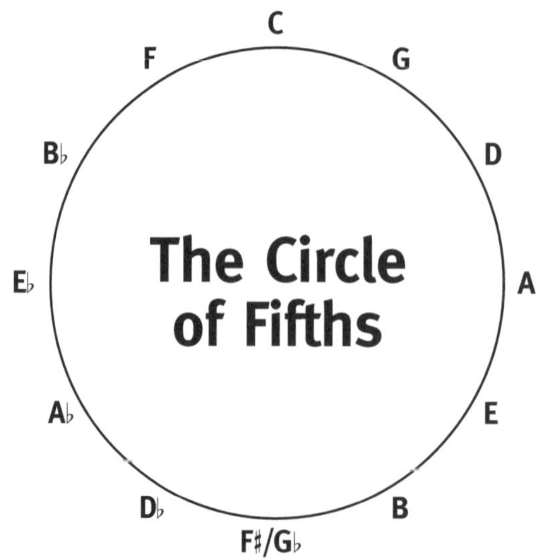

As you can see, by starting at 12 o'clock, the first scale is C, which has already been covered. You can then move around the circle in either clockwise or anti-clockwise directions, playing through the scales as you go. I recommend going clockwise for now.

In the exercise on the next page you'll find the sequence of all 12 keys, which you can also hear on the CD. Each key is separated by a bar's rest in order to give you time to prepare for the next scale. I suggest playing through this exercise at least every other day, if not every day. You should find it quite easy to follow, since the fretboard shape you learnt back on Day 23 applies to all keys. Keep an eye on the tab if you're unsure and play along with the CD; you'll then be able to hear if you go wrong.

DAY 30 STUDY

1. Practise the major-scale exercise presented today.

2. Try to remember the sequence of keys. (It will be useful to know as your playing advances.)

Exercise 45

♩ = 80

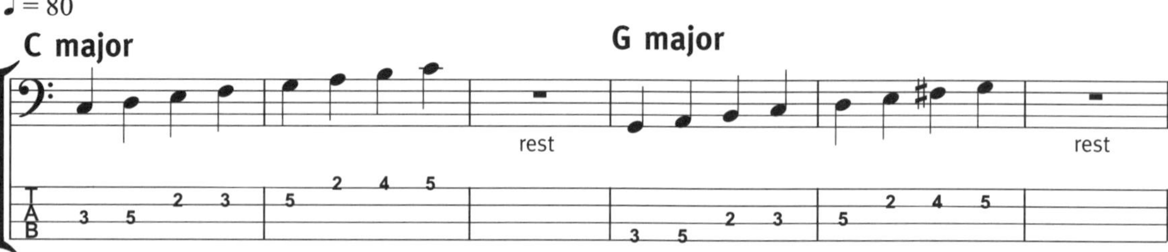

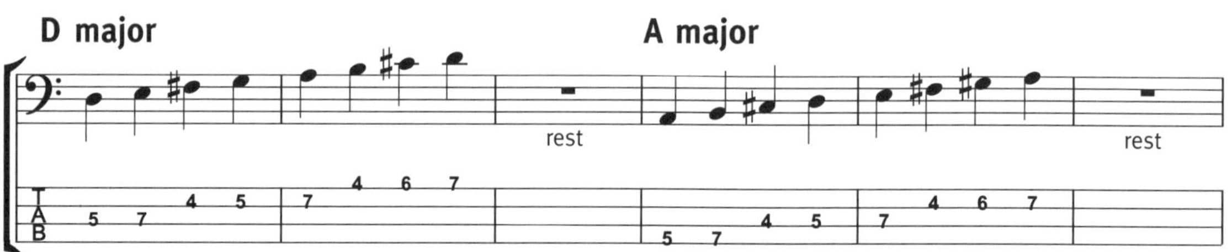

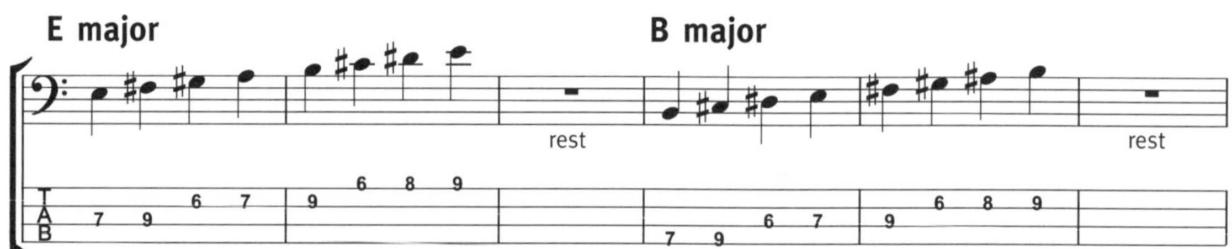

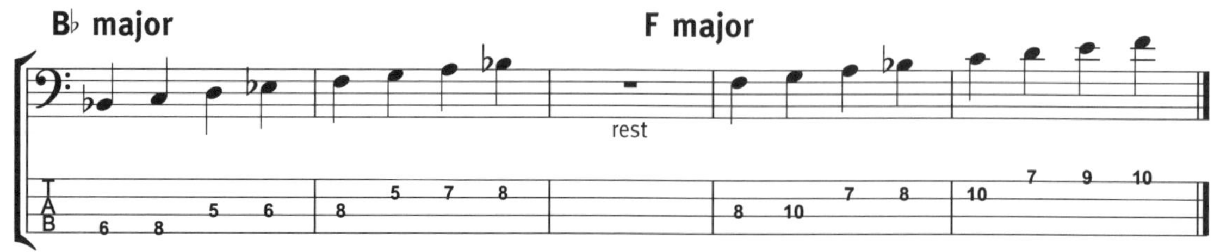

DAY 31: TIES AND DOTTED RHYTHMS

Your goal for Day 31 is to learn about ties and dotted rhythms and how to read them.

So far we've looked at note values that last for one beat, two beats, four beats and half a beat. But what happens if we want a note that lasts for, say, a beat and a half? Or two and a half beats? In order to notate rhythms like this, there are two tools available to us: ties or dots. Today we will look at how both methods are used and examine some simple basslines that illustrate these elements.

TIES

A tie is a curved line that connects two notes, signifying that the played note continues for the duration of the note it's tied to as well. Lets take the first example mentioned above and look at how to use a tie to write a note that lasts for a beat and a half. This would be written as a quarter note (a beat) and an eighth note (a half-beat). Tying two the together creates a note that lasts for a beat and a half:

In the example above, the first note lasts for a beat and a half and is followed by an eighth note on the 'and' of beat two. This is a very common rhythm in popular music.

Let's look now at how we would notate the same thing using a dotted note.

DOTTED NOTES

Adding a dot after a note means that its value is increased by 50%. Therefore, a dotted quarter note lasts for one and a half beats. Similarly, a dotted half note lasts for three beats. Below I've written the same bass part as before, but this time using a dotted note:

This rhythm is notated more often with a dot than a tie – you might agree that it's easier to read.

Today we've now covered the basic theory of dots and ties, so let's finish things off by looking at three bass parts that use a combination of these methods. Remember, you aren't expected to sight-read these bass parts as such, merely to study them for future reference.

Bass

PRACTICAL EXERCISE

This bassline uses the dotted quarter-note/eighth-note figure we've just looked at. As I said, it's a very common rhythmic figure and should sound familiar.

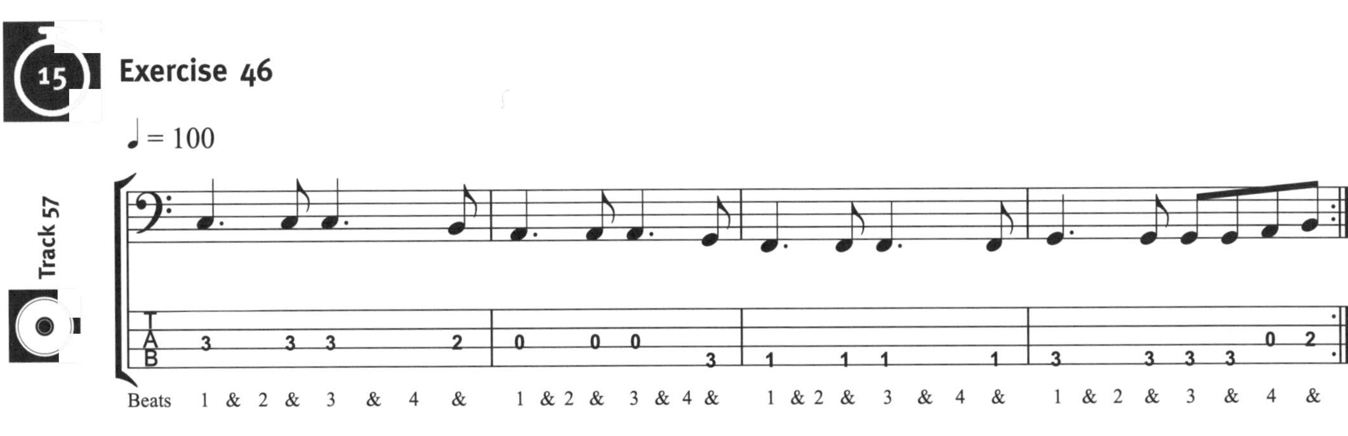

PRACTICAL EXERCISE

This bassline features a mixture of dotted notes and ties. Follow the beat guidelines beneath the stave to see exactly where each note is played.

DAY 31 STUDY

1 Learn the basslines presented in today's lesson.

2 Study some printed music to see how dotted rhythms and ties are used. Try to work out how they would sound.

DAY 32: MORE PHRASING TOOLS

Your goal for Day 31 is to learn how to use three new phrasing tools: trills, vibrato and string bends.

We've already looked at three important phrasing techniques: the hammer-on, pull-off and the slide. It's time now to introduce you to the last three that we will look at in this book: trills, vibrato and string bending. You may have heard of them before – all three are very popular with guitarists.

TRILLS

The first phrasing tool we're going to look at is the trill. Trills are best described as successive hammer-ons and pull-offs played quickly. (You can hear a trill on Track 59 of the CD, played slowly and then accelerating for full effect.) Like all phrasing techniques, trills can add flavour to your basslines if used sparingly. When playing a trill, only the first note is struck; the rest of the notes are played by hammering on and pulling off quickly. Also, only the first note and trill note are actually written, with the trill notated by the letters 'tr' followed by a wavy line. Here's an exercises that makes use of trills:

VIBRATO

The vibrato technique involves wobbling the string up and down slightly in order to create variations in the pitch of the note. (On Track 60 you can hear an exaggerated example of this.) Vibrato is indicated by a wavy line over the note in question. The next bassline is an example of how to use the technique effectively:

STRING BENDING

The string-bending technique involves...wait for it...bending the strings! Doing so raises the pitch of the played note by a degree determined by how far you bend the string. It's possible to produce some really cool effects with string bending.

Track 61

To bend a string, simply pull down on it, or push it upwards. The change in the tension of the string raises the pitch of the note. You can hear me bending the strings on the CD.

Bass

There are two types of string bends: the bend and the bend and release. The bend involves playing the string and bending it as discussed, a manoeuvre indicated by a small arrow with a number above it. If you see '1/2' written above a bend, it means you should bend the string up to the pitch of the note a semitone (or one fret) away. If you see 'full', you should bend the string up the pitch of the note a full tone (two frets) away. A bend and release involves bending the string up, then releasing it back to the original note. Here's an exercise that uses both types of bend:

Exercise 50

Remember that, while these techniques can be a lot of fun, they should be used sparingly. They're much more effective this way.

DAY 32 STUDY

1 Learn the techniques and bass parts introduced in this section.

2 Try to incorporate these techniques into your repertoire. Maybe you can come up with some lines of your own that use them.

DAY 33: INTRODUCING THE MINOR SCALE

Your goal for Day 33 is to learn how to play the minor scale.

We've already looked at the major scale and its construction, and hopefully by now you're practising all 12 major scales as part of your practice routine. It's time now to learn about the minor scale, which is just as important as the major in Western music. When you play through the minor scale, though, you'll notice that it sounds very different. Straight away, you'll hear that the minor scale doesn't sound quite as cheerful as its major counterpart. In simple terms, the minor scale sounds 'sad', whereas the major scale sounds 'happy.'

Here's an A minor scale. Play through it a few times just to get the sound of it into your head, and be sure to keep an eye on the fingering guide written between the staves.

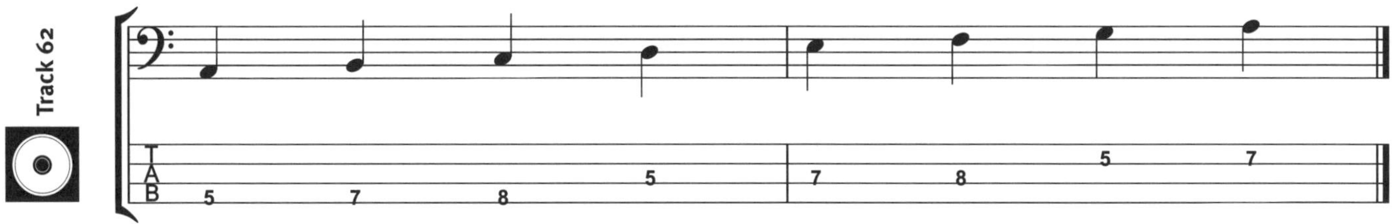

Over the page is a fretboard representation of the minor scale. The black dots represent the root (A) and its octave:

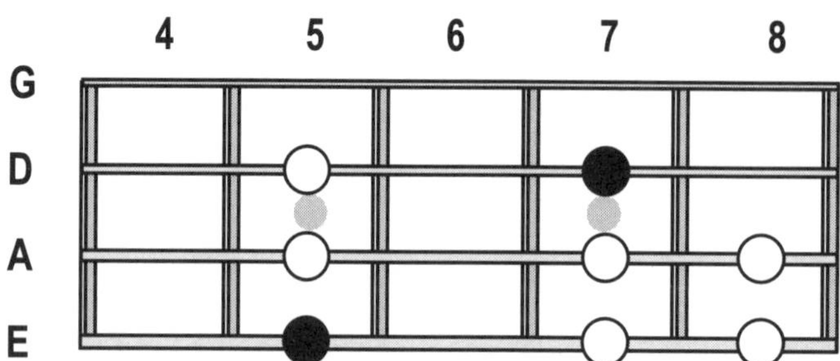

As with the major scales, fretboard patterns such as these are completely moveable – for example, you could play this pattern from the G on your E string, which would result in a G minor scale.

RELATIVE MINORS

You might have noticed that the A minor scale contains the notes A, B, C, D, E, F, G and A – all naturals. This was also the case with the scale of C major. Therefore, you could convincingly argue that C major and A minor are the same scale, just starting on different notes. This is completely true. We actually say that they are *related*, since they contain the same notes. Every major scale consequently has a *relative minor* – C major's is A minor. To find the relative minor scale of any major scale, simply count up to the sixth note:

C	D	E	F	G	(A)	B	C
1	2	3	4	5	(6)	7	8

I recommend practising the minor scale in different places on the fretboard. When you're happy with the fingering pattern, try playing through all 12 scales, following the pattern on the circle-of-fifths diagram from Day 30.

THE INTERVALS OF THE MINOR SCALE

When we looked at major scales, I introduced you to intervals and showed you how the major scale is created from a specific arrangement of tones and semitones. The minor scale is similar, although it does have a different sequence of intervals. Here is a diagram of the minor scale with the pattern of intervals from which it is created:

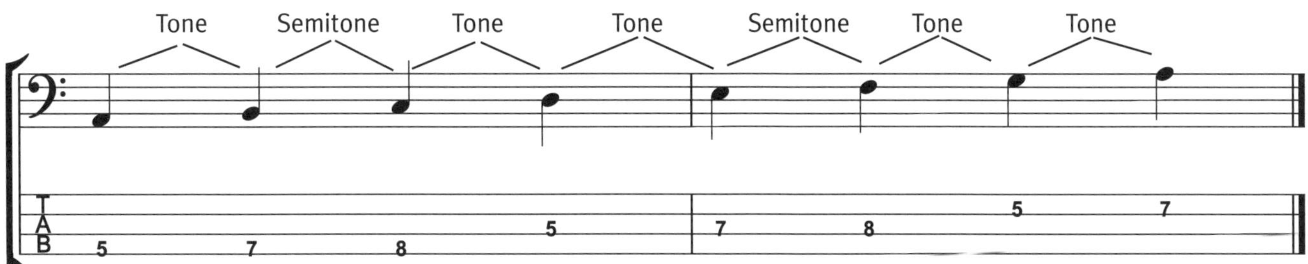

As you can see, the pattern that defines a minor scale is tone, semitone, tone, tone, semitone, tone, tone, or TSTTSTT.

Again, there's a lot of information to swallow this week, but if you've been working on your major scales as suggested, you should find it relatively straightforward. Be sure that you don't rush through your minor scales – make sure you have the A minor scale under your fingers before you attempt to play it in other keys.

Using the information from this week's study, you should be able to play a minor scale in any key.

DAY 33 STUDY

1 Practise the A minor scale.

2 When you're happy with the A minor scale, practise it in other keys. When you're confident with this, try playing all 12 following the pattern dictated by the circle of fifths.

DAY 34: CORE TOPIC – DISCO BASSLINES

Your goal for Day 34 is to learn another couple of disco basslines.

Today we'll continue to look at the disco style I introduced at the beginning of the week. Disco basslines are quite challenging compared to some of the others you've learnt so far, so take them slowly.

QUOTE FOR THE DAY

I think drummers like to play with me because I make them sound good. That is the function of the bass player.

– Jack Bruce

PRACTICAL EXERCISE

This bassline makes use of space. Note how every second bar moves things along with the use of octaves.

Exercise 51

♩ = 110

Bass

PRACTICAL EXERCISE

You'll notice the use of octaves again in this line, but by now you can no doubt hear that they are integral to this style of music.

Exercise 52

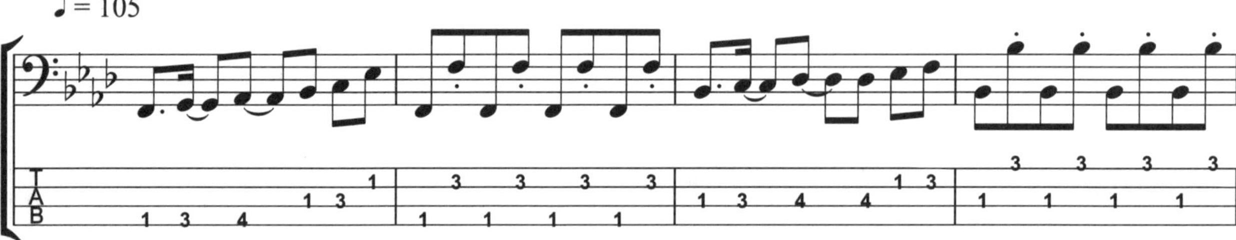

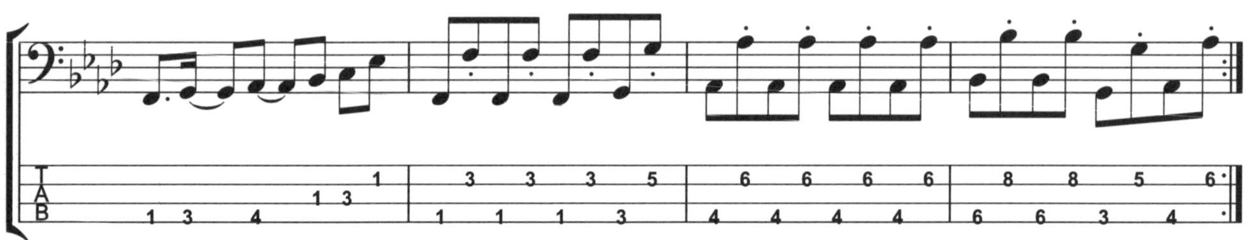

When learning a new style, it's very important to listen to as much relevant music as possible. As a starting point, I recommend the following tracks, all of which feature great bass parts:

Sister Sledge: 'We Are Family'

Gloria Gaynor: 'I Will Survive'

McFadden And Whitehead: 'Ain't No Stoppin' Us Now'

The Trammps: 'Disco Inferno'

The Bee Gees: 'Stayin' Alive'

A Taste Of Honey: 'Boogie Oogie Oogie'

Jocelyn Brown: 'Somebody Else's Guy'

The Whispers: 'And The Beat Goes On'

Chic: 'Le Freak'

Rose Royce: 'Carwash'

DAY 34 STUDY

1 Practise the two exercises from this section. Take them slow to begin with and refer to the CD to get them just right.

2 Listen to some disco music. All of these bass parts will make more sense if you've listened to examples from the style.

3 Make sure that you understand everything covered this week. Tomorrow is another test day!

Bass

DAY 35

WEEK 5 TEST

Today is your fifth test day. As before, you should complete this test before moving on. Everything you need to know was covered in the previous week.

1 What effect does adding a dot after a note have on the length of the note?

2 What are ties used for?

3 What is a trill?

4 If '1/2' was written over a string bend, to what pitch would you bend the note?

5 What is meant by the term 'relative minor scale'?

6 Which scale is the relative minor of C major?

7 What sequence of tones and semitones makes up a minor scale?

8 Name some of the characteristics of a disco bassline.

9 Which note is found at the sixth fret on the D string?

10 Which note is found at the fourth fret on the E string?

TIMED EXERCISE

Finally, here is another new bassline for you to study. You should be able to get it down in about 30 minutes. This pattern is comprised entirely of octaves, which, as I mentioned at the beginning of the week, play a vital role in disco basslines and are an important tool to have under your belt. You'll notice that the staccato marks are also present again.

WEEK 6

OVERVIEW

A new style this week: rock music. Like pop music, rock music is quite a broad genre, but hopefully by the end of the week you'll understand the style a little better. We're also going to continue to develop what you've so far learnt about scales and music notation. Here's a full breakdown of what we'll be looking at this week:

- **Core Topic: Rock Music** – This week we're going to take a look at rock music, including a brief history and four typical rock basslines.

- **Major Scale Triads** – Now that you're familiar with the major scale, it's time to take a look at the chords that can be created from it.

- **Music Notation** – This week we'll look at 16th-note rhythms. This is where things get nasty!

- **Using A Pick** – Since we're looking at rock music this week, we're also going to look at how to play with a pick – very popular in rock music!

- **Arpeggios** – Once you've studied the triads of the major scale, it's time to learn to play them as arpeggios. What's an arpeggio? You'll find out!

DAY 36: CORE TOPIC – ROCK MUSIC

Your goal for Day 36 is to learn about rock music and to play some typical rock basslines.

QUOTE FOR THE DAY

There really isn't much of a difference, other than the notes that you play, as long as you understand the genre that you're in.

– *Stanley Clarke*

Rock music as we know it today originally evolved from the blues in the early 1960s, allowing bands such as Cream, The Rolling Stones and Led Zeppelin to become three of the most important acts in musical history. As the years went on, rock evolved into a harder, more aggressive sound with acts like KISS, Cheap Trick, Whitesnake and Poison becoming hugely successful in the '70s and '80s. Rock also diversified into many key areas, one of these being heavy metal, which produced enduringly popular groups such as Metallica, Iron Maiden, Megadeth and many more. Over the last 20 years, rock has continued to evolve, and new influences have been added along the way. This has culminated in what we know today as nu metal, a modern rock style led by bands such as Korn, Limp Bizkit, Linkin Park and Papa Roach.

Rock music differs from pop and disco music in several ways. It is generally typified by the use of heavily distorted guitars, simpler chord progressions (most of the time) and a much more aggressive attitude. The bass guitar's role in rock music is in many ways a simpler role than in pop, with static, pumping, pick-played lines being quite often the order of the day.

Today we'll look at three rock basslines that are representative of the style.

Bass

PRACTICAL EXERCISE

This exercise features a classic rock chord progression. Notice how the bass remains the same underneath the chord changes – this creates tension. A line such as this would work well for a verse part, with the tension resolved on the chorus by having the bass follow the chord progression more closely.

Exercise 53

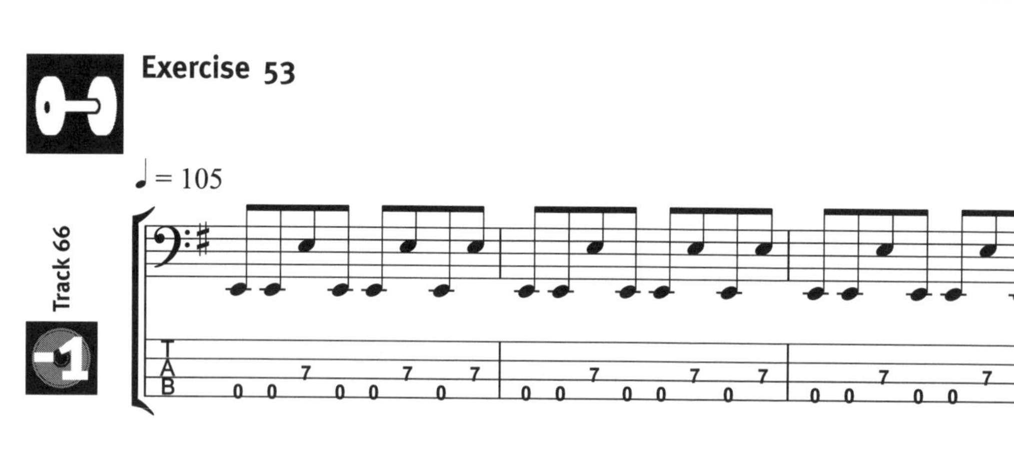

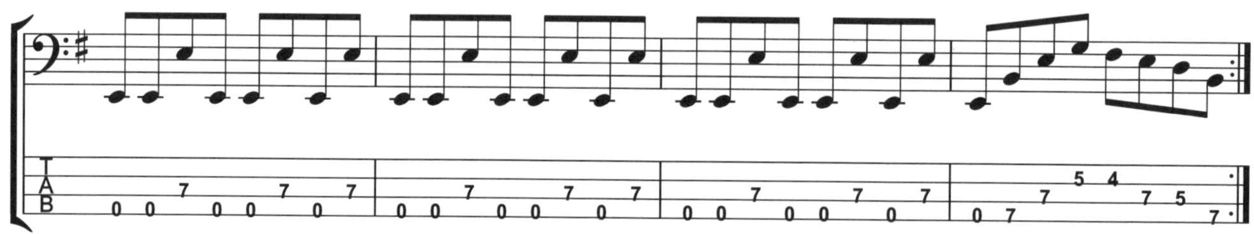

PRACTICAL EXERCISE

This next exercise is a slower, bluesier number that has a more eventful bassline, one that more closely follows the guitar part. Note the small chromatic figures on beats 3 and 4 of the first bar, and the accented figures at the end of the fourth bar. All are classic rock elements, as is the use of the descending blues scale from the second half of bar 2.

Bass

Exercise 54

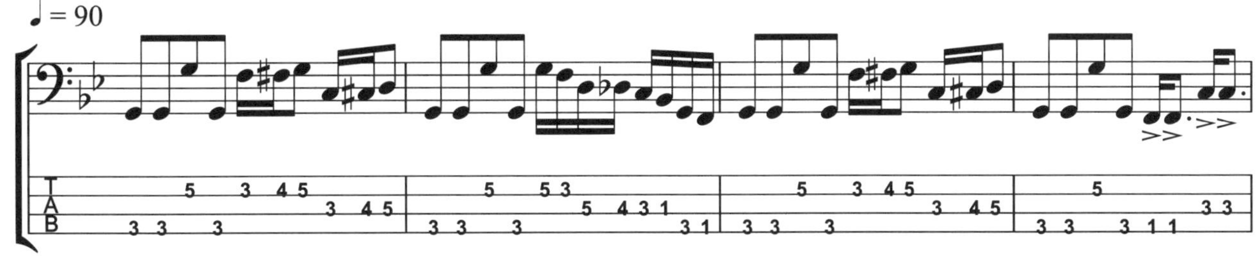

DAY 36 STUDY

1 Begin learning the three rock basslines that we've just looked at. Continue to practise these during the course of the coming week.

Bass

DAY 37: TRIADS OF THE MAJOR SCALE

Your goals for Day 37 are:

- To understand what a triad is;
- To discover how triads can be built using the major scale.

QUOTE FOR THE DAY

Harmony and theory can be useful if you're thinking of writing tunes.

– Laurence Cottle

As bass players, most of you will be seeking the capability of playing along with other musicians and being able to create your own bass parts. Having a good working knowledge of chords and the notes found within any chord will help you significantly in realizing this goal. To this end, today we're going to look at triads, the most basic types of chord. All of the chords covered today are going to be built on the C major scale, which you should already know.

As the name suggests, triads are built out of three notes: root, third and fifth. In the case of a C major triad, these notes would be C (the root), E (the third note of the scale) and G (the fifth). You can probably see a pattern from the illustration below – every other note has been missed out.

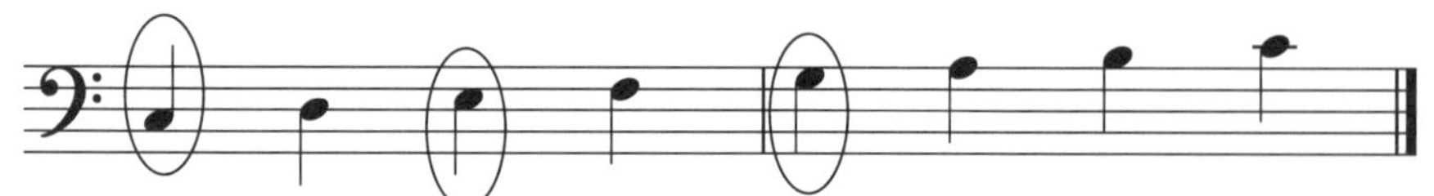

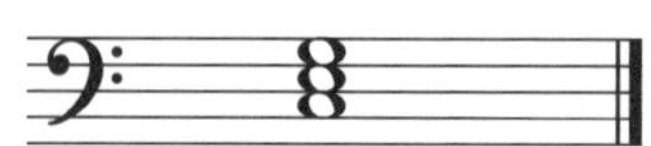

Track 68

Major chords are built out of intervals known as *thirds*. In the example above, the distance between the C and E – four semitones – is known as a *major third*. This is the interval that defines the chord and give it its major sound. The interval between the E and G – three semitones – is known as a *minor third*. Therefore, a major chord is made up of a major third and a minor third:

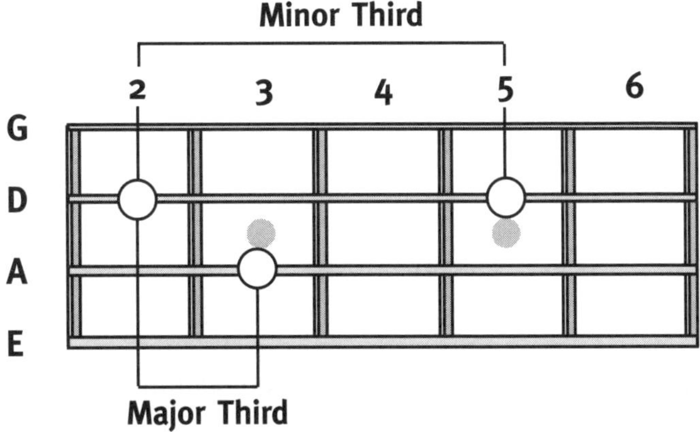

Using this knowledge, we can now build triads on each degree of the C major scale. First, let's build a triad from the second note, D. Using D as the first note and counting up, the third note will be F and the fifth will be A. Playing these notes together will produce a different sound from the C major chord, however. This is because we've created a D minor chord.

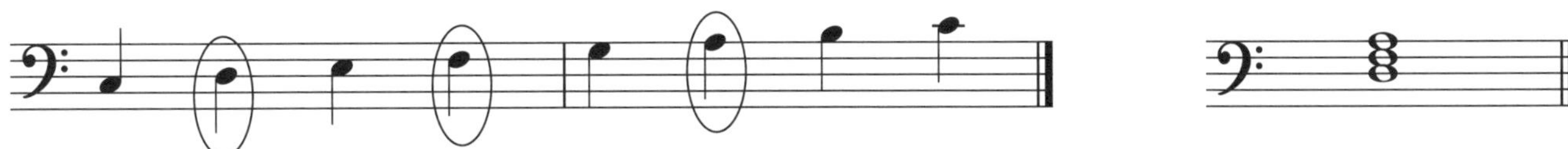

A minor chord is created from a different set of intervals from its respective major, specifically a minor third followed by a major third, as shown over the page:

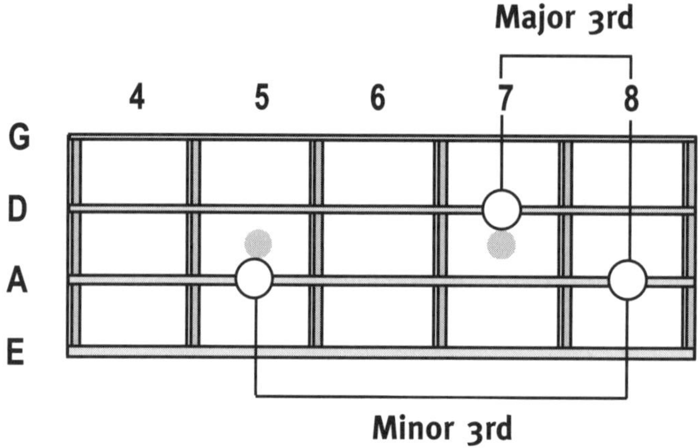

This is the essence of diatonic harmony. Building chords in thirds from each note of the scale will yield a combination of both major and minor chords. Notice, however, that both major and minor chords contain the interval of the perfect fifth: C to G and D to A. This interval is present in all major and minor chords:

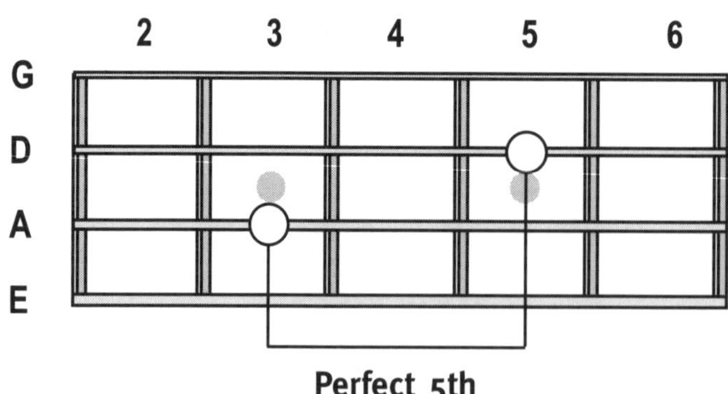

Here are all the triads that can be created from the C major scale (note that from G onwards the notes are shown an octave lower so that they can be kept on the stave).

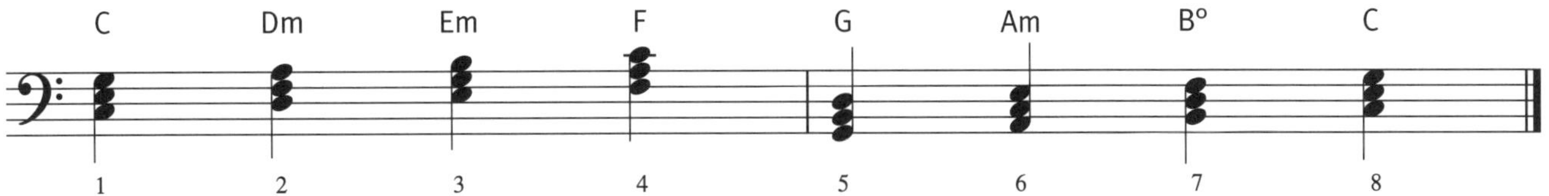

You'll notice that the chords built on the first, fourth and fifth degrees are major. These are chords on which the 12-bar blues and many pop songs are based. The chords on the second, third and sixth degrees are minor chords, which leaves us with just one last chord: the B diminished chord, built from the seventh degree. Diminished chords are often indicated by a ° sign.

The chord built on the seventh degree of any major scale is always a diminished chord. Diminished chords have a very distinctive (and rather unpleasant) sound and are built up of a unique set of intervals: a minor third plus another minor third.

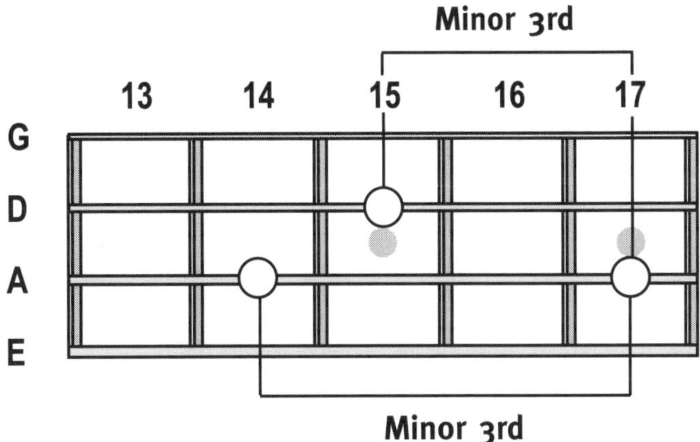

We've now looked at all three chord types available from the simple major scale. Today I've introduced you to many new concepts, and it's important that you re-read through this information a few times in order to digest it thoroughly. We'll continue our look at triads in a few days' time.

DAY 37 STUDY

1 Be sure that you understand the information presented in this section.

2 Which intervals form a major chord?

3 Which intervals form a minor chord?

4 Which intervals form a diminished chord?

DAY 38: 16th NOTES

Your goal for Day 38 is to learn about 16th notes and how to read them.

We've now looked at many different note values, from whole and half notes to quarter and eighth notes. We've also seen that we can extend a note's value by 50% by placing a dot after it and that two notes can be joined by a tie.

Today we are going to look at *16th notes*, or *semiquavers*. These are probably the toughest customers you'll ever have to read, because they go by pretty quickly. Add to that the ways in which they can be grouped with other note values and you're looking at some difficult reading. For now, though, we're just going to look at groups of 16th notes (we'll look at the other possible rhythmic pairings next week).

A 16th note lasts for a quarter of a beat. That means that for every beat, or foot-tap, you can play four notes. In a bar of 4/4, there are potentially 16 16th notes. In the example below – which is also recorded on the CD – you can see and hear how they sound. (Bear in mind that these have been recorded at a relatively slow tempo.)

Bass

16ths can be tricky to count, and it's useful to have a vocal mnemonic to help in this. Imagine saying the word 'Coca-Cola'; this is a four syllable word that accurately demonstrates how a group of four 16th notes should sound. Practise playing the next exercise and saying 'Coca-Cola' along with it.

Exercise 55

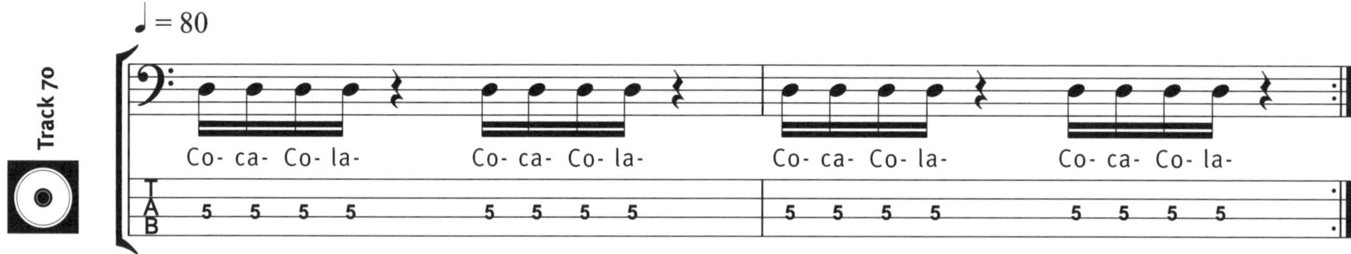

RESTS

Introducing 16th-note rests into the equation can make things a little complicated. To illustrate this, here are a few lines that incorporate rests.

In this first example, the first 16th note of each beat is replaced with a rest. As you play through it, try to imagine the first syllable of the word, but don't play it:

Exercise 56

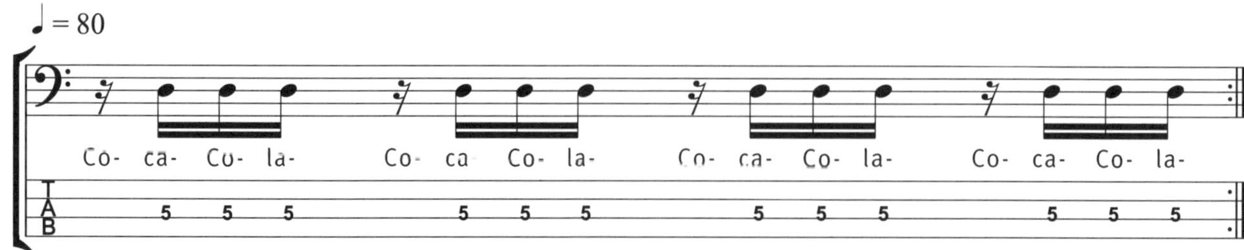

This next example will be a little easier, as all you have to do is omit the last 16th note of each beat:

Exercise 57

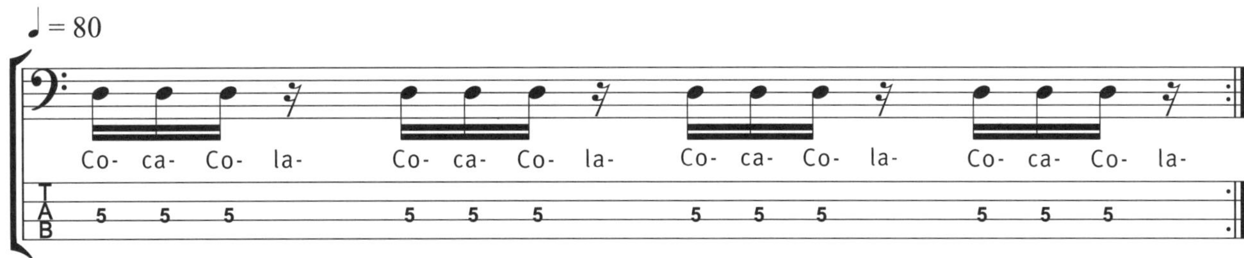

We'll take a further look at 16th-note exercises next week. For now, though, I advise you to practise what we've covered in today's lesson and be sure that you understand and are able to play the exercises before moving on.

DAY 38 STUDY

1 Practise all of the 16th-note exercises in this section.

2 Look through some music books and look for 16th notes and their rests. See if you can work out how they should sound.

DAY 39: USING A PICK

Your goal for Day 39 is to understand how to use a pick to play the bass.

QUOTE FOR THE DAY

Sometimes you might want to use a pick for a more twangy sound.

– Chris Wolstenholme, Muse

Using a pick, or *plectrum*, to play the bass is very popular in rock music, hence its inclusion this week. Rock players generally prefer the pick, as it produces a heavier, punchier sound than the fingers, because the attack produced by the plastic of the plectrum striking the string cannot be reproduced with the tips of the fingers. Pick-playing is also a more aggressive style, one that you can literally put your entire arm into, especially if you wear your bass low, as many rock players do. You might also notice pick players wearing sweatbands on their wrists, particularly for the picking hand; this is mainly to protect the skin from the constant abrasion against the edge of the bass or the bridge, as shown below:

HOW TO USE A PICK

As you can see from the photograph on the previous page, the pick is held between the first finger and thumb of the right hand. As you pluck the strings, it's helpful to rest the wrist of your right hand on either the bridge or body of the bass in order to provide a stable anchor point from which to play. There are many different ways to play using a pick – some bassists, for example, will use mostly downstrokes (an approach favoured by renowned heavy-metal bassist Jason Newsted) while others will use a combination of down- and upstrokes. Which technique you use depends on the tempo of the song; at slow tempos it's relatively easy to use just downstrokes, but at fast rock tempos of 140bpm upwards you're going to need both. You should practise playing with both up- and downstrokes, as this will enable you to play cleaner and faster, and indeed speed is the main advantage that pick playing has over fingerstyle. It's possible to play continuous 16th notes at very high speeds using a pick, something that would tire the hands of even the most experienced fingerstyle player. Having said that, it's very difficult to cross strings (particularly more than one) when playing with a pick.

Throughout the following exercises, I've notated picking guides between the staves:

Downstroke = ⊓ **Upstroke =** V

In this first example, you'll be playing a continuous eighth-note line using both down- and upstrokes:

Bass

Exercise 58

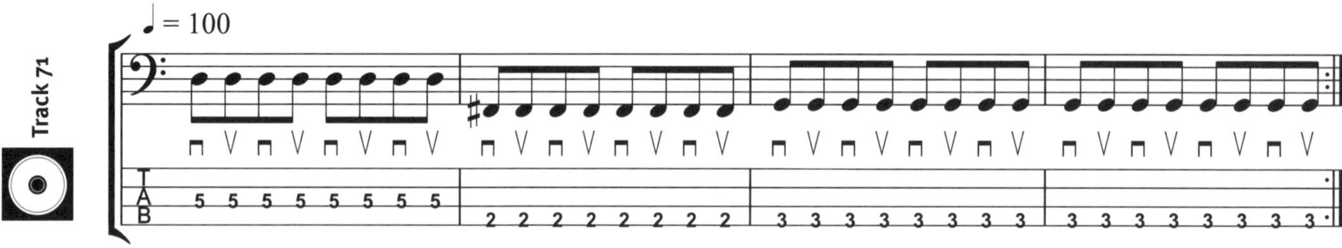

As the bass part is so sparse, and you need to cross strings, this next line can be played with downstrokes only:

Exercise 59

The next line features a 16th-note groove, and you'll need to use a strict combination of up- and downstrokes in order to execute it correctly. When you hear this exercise, it might seem like a big step from the previous exercises, but the principle of strict up- and downstrokes remains the same. Take your time and don't worry if you find you need to spend more time on this one:

Exercise 60

Many people think that they can play either with their fingers or with a pick.

Remember that there's no reason why you shouldn't learn to do both.

DAY 39 STUDY

1 What are the benefits of playing with a pick?

2 What are the drawbacks?

3 Why does pick playing suit rock music?

4 Practise the three exercises introduced in this section.

DAY 40: TRIADS (CONTINUED)

Your goals for Day 40 are:

- To understand what an arpeggio is;
- To use arpeggios to play the triads derived from a major scale.

A few days ago we looked at the triads that can be built from the C major scale. Now it's time for you to learn how to play them. To this end, we're going to play them as *arpeggios*. The words *chord* and *triad* imply that all of the notes in question should be played together, as they would be on a guitar or keyboard. As bass players, we won't be playing chords too often – at least, not in the way that your bandmates will. Instead, we'll be playing chords one note at a time. In doing so, we're playing arpeggios. For example, if you played the notes of a C major chord one after the other – C, E and G – you'd have played a C major arpeggio.

Over the page are all of the chords found in the key of C major written as arpeggios. You'll see that in the case of each chord I've added the octave; this will allow you to stay comfortably in 4/4 time:

Bass

Exercise 61

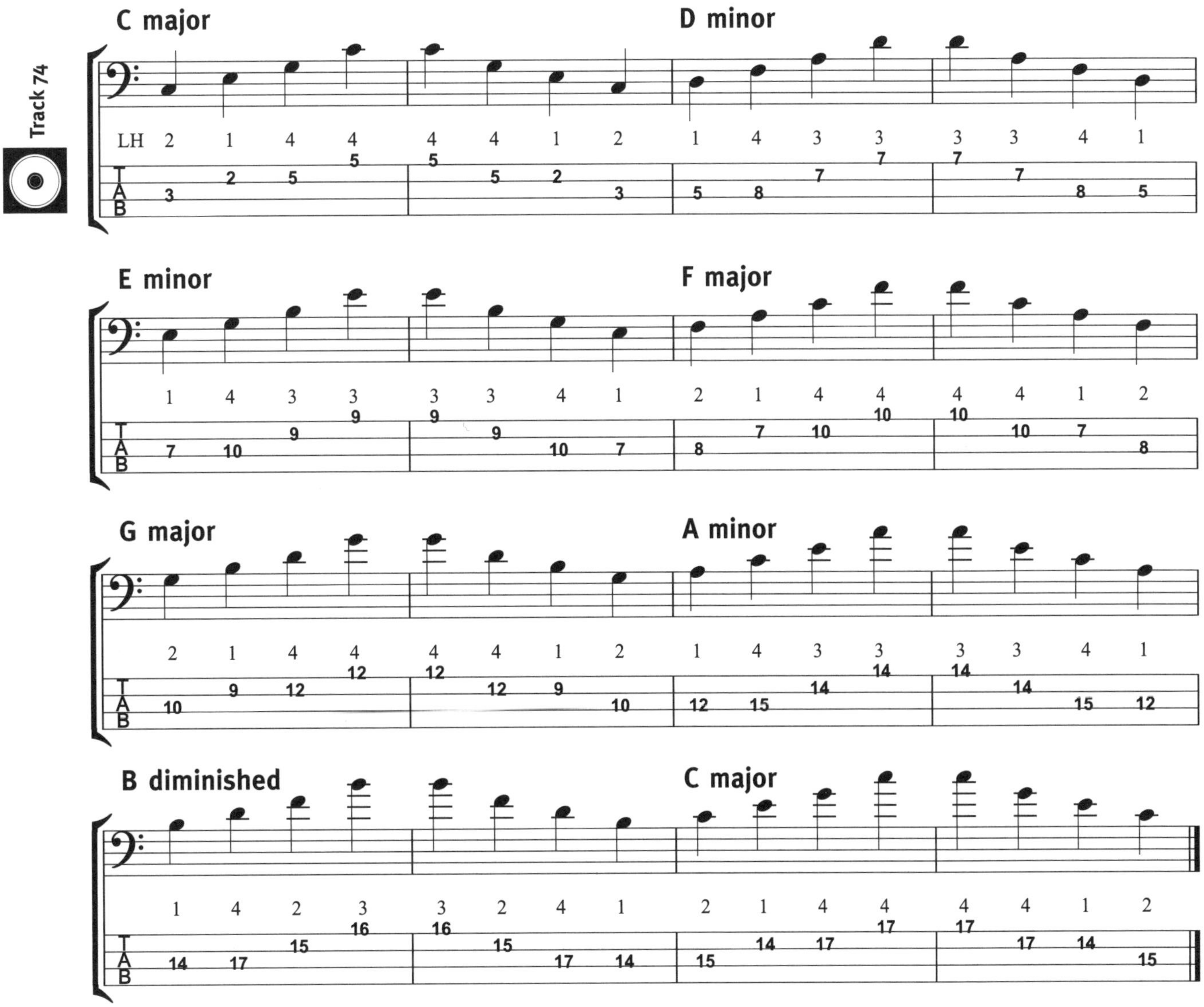

Track 74

C major

LH 2 1 4 4 | 4 4 1 2

TAB: 3 2 5 5 | 5 5 2 3

D minor

1 4 3 3 | 3 3 4 1

TAB: 5 8 7 7 | 7 7 8 5

E minor

1 4 3 3 | 3 3 4 1

TAB: 7 10 9 9 | 9 9 10 7

F major

2 1 4 4 | 4 4 1 2

TAB: 8 7 10 10 | 10 10 7 8

G major

2 1 4 4 | 4 4 1 2

TAB: 10 9 12 12 | 12 12 9 10

A minor

1 4 3 3 | 3 3 4 1

TAB: 12 15 14 14 | 14 14 15 12

B diminished

1 4 2 3 | 3 2 4 1

TAB: 14 17 15 16 | 16 15 17 14

C major

2 1 4 4 | 4 4 1 2

TAB: 15 14 17 17 | 17 17 14 15

Pay close attention to the left-hand guides notated between the staves. They are the most sensible fingering choices available to you.

This sequence of chords will work in any of the 12 major keys. Once you know your scales, you could write out any scale and then work out the chords available from it using the knowledge you've acquired this week.

MINOR KEY TRIADS AND ARPEGGIOS

Since you know that C major is related to the key of A minor, by playing through these triads you're also playing the triads that would be created from an A minor scale!

DAY 40 STUDY

1 What is an arpeggio?

2 Learn the arpeggio exercise introduced in this section.

Bass

DAY 41: CORE TOPIC – ROCK BASSLINES

Your goal for Day 41 is to further your knowledge of rock bass parts.

Finally for this week, we're going to look at two more basslines that illustrate the rock style. As you've now has a go at playing with a pick, feel free to try these and any of the previous exercises with a pick.

QUOTE FOR THE DAY

My sensibilities over the years have always been influenced by the whole evolution of bass. I've studied the history of the bass through jazz and rock and continue to study it by listening to different players and composers.

– *Mark Egan*

PRACTICAL EXERCISE

The exercise on the next page is in the '70s rock style. Notice how the bass and guitar play the riff in unison – very common in music. Also worth a mention are the string bends in bars 2 and 4 and the upper-register fills in bars 6 and 8 – very reminiscent of the playing of John Paul Jones (Led Zeppelin), Geezer Butler (Black Sabbath) and Gene Simmons (KISS).

PRACTICAL EXERCISE

This exercise has more of a funk-rock feel. These kinds of grooves were also popular in the '70s and were used by bands such as Aerosmith and Cheap Trick.

Here's a small list of songs that I recommend checking out:

Led Zeppelin: 'Black Dog'

KISS: 'Cold Gin'

Black Sabbath: 'Paranoid'

Iron Maiden: 'Run To The Hills'

Aerosmith: 'Walk This Way'

Metallica: 'Enter Sandman'

Incubus: 'Are You In'

Rage Against The Machine: 'Bombtrack'

Papa Roach: 'Last Resort'

Limp Bizkit: 'Take A Look Around'

DAY 41 STUDY

1 Practise the two rock bassline introduced today, as well as the three we looked at on day 36.

2 Make sure you understand everything covered this week. Tomorrow is another big test day!

Bass

DAY 42

WEEK 6 TEST

Today is your sixth test day. As before, you should complete this test before moving on. Everything you need to know was covered last week.

---

1 Which two intervals make up a major triad?

2 Which two intervals make up a minor triad?

3 Which two intervals make up a diminished triad?

4 What is an arpeggio?

5 What's the difference between a triad and an arpeggio?

6 Name some of the characteristics of rock music.

7 What are the benefits of playing with a pick?

8 How many 16th notes is it possible to have in a bar of 4/4?

9 What is the UK terminology for a 16th note?

10 Which note is found at the second fret on the G string?

TIMED EXERCISE

Finally, here's another new rock bassline for you to study. You should aim to be able to play this one within 30 minutes. This exercise contains a driving eighth-note line very typical of the rock style. Note how each chord is anticipated by the eighth note preceding it.

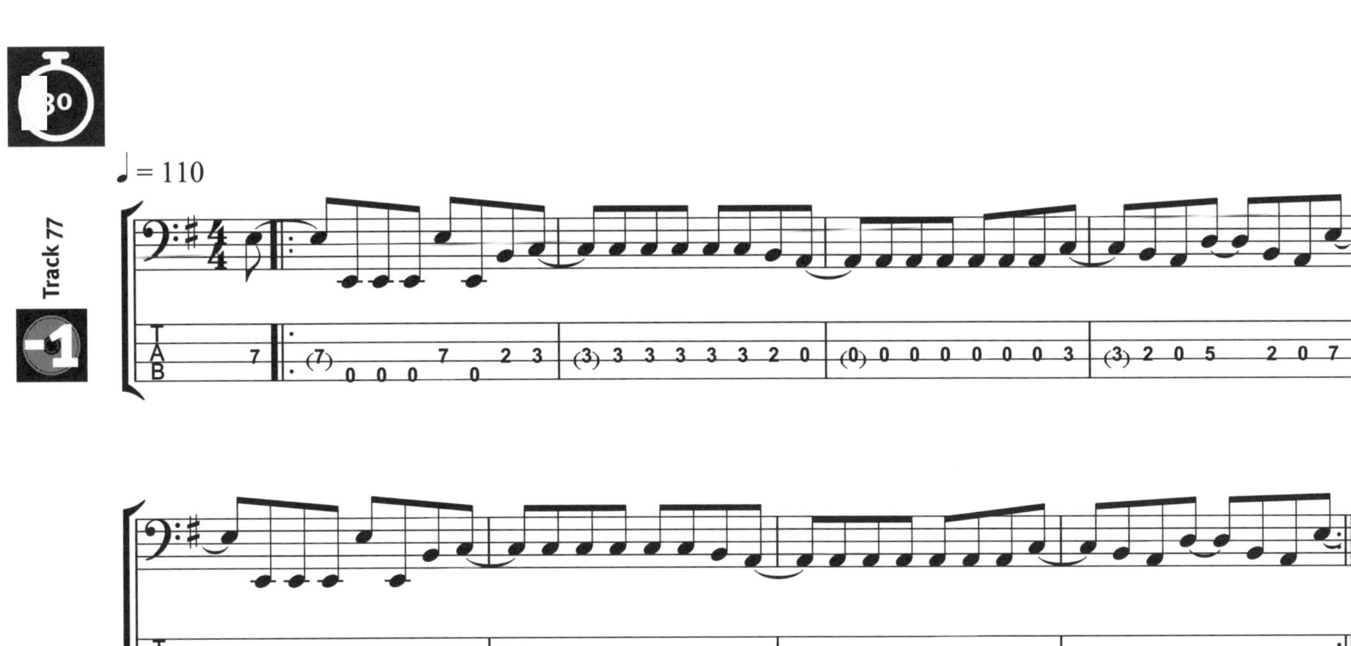

WEEK 7

OVERVIEW

You should have the basic elements of several different styles of music under your belt by now. This week we're going to look at a new style: reggae. We'll also be continuing to look at scales and music notation, including more 16th notes. Here's a full breakdown of what we'll be looking at in the coming week:

- **Core Topic: Reggae Music** – Like I said, this week's core genre will be reggae. We'll cover a brief history and four typical reggae basslines.

- **The Major Pentatonic Scale** – We're also going to look at a simpler scale that's comparatively easy to get to grips with: the pentatonic scale.

- **Music Notation** – If you thought last week's look at 16th notes was nasty, you're in for a shock! This week we'll take a look at how to combine them with other rhythms.

- **Ghost Notes** – What they are and how to use them.

- **Dynamics** – Dynamics are important to any musician, and this week we'll look at which ones will help you improve your playing.

DAY 43: CORE TOPIC – REGGAE MUSIC

Your goal for Day 43 is to learn about reggae music and play some typical reggae basslines.

Reggae is a style of music that originated in Jamaica, although its roots can be traced back to Africa, the Jamaican slaves' homeland. Its origins can be heard in ska music, which was popular in the '60s and remains so to this day. Reggae is a slower, more soulful variation of ska music characterised by 'skanking' guitar rhythms, usually played on semiquaver upbeats. Reggae was brought to worldwide attention by Bob Marley and his band The Wailers, who had many hits during their time together.

QUOTE FOR THE DAY

I think we [Dream Theater] are good at what we do. At the same time, we're not blind to other styles of music, so it's all relative to not so much being great at everything as it is finding your niche.

– John Myung, Dream Theater

Let's look at some typical reggae basslines.

PRACTICAL EXERCISE

The bassline at the top of the next page is classic reggae. Note the semiquaver (16th-note) upbeats on the second half of the first beat of the first four bars. Also, on beat 3 note the use of triplets, which are popular in reggae – you can hear good examples of these on 'Message In A Bottle' by The Police.

Bass

Exercise 64

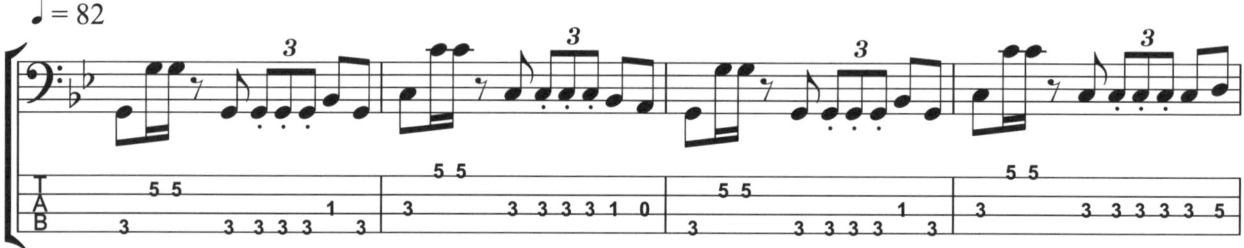

PRACTICAL EXERCISE

This next bass part has a descending melodic bass figure that's quite ear-catching. Note that both lines have very simple chord progressions – another characteristic of reggae.

Exercise 65

DAY 43 STUDY

1 Practise the three reggae basslines presented here. Continue to work on them throughout the week.

2 Name some of the characteristics of reggae music.

Bass

DAY 44: THE MAJOR PENTATONIC SCALE

Your goal for Day 44 is to learn the major pentatonic scale and how to practise it.

Over the last few weeks we've looked at major and minor scales, and by now you might be groaning at the thought of learning another scale. Well, fear not! This scale is based on the major scale, and is even simpler. Even better, it's a very useful scale and one that you'll probably want to start using straight away. It has quite a familiar sound and is the guitarist's and bassist's best friend. I am, of course, talking about the pentatonic scale.

The *pentatonic* derives its name from the Greek word *penta*, meaning 'five', which is certainly an appropriate name, as the scale has only five notes in it – well, six if you count the octave.

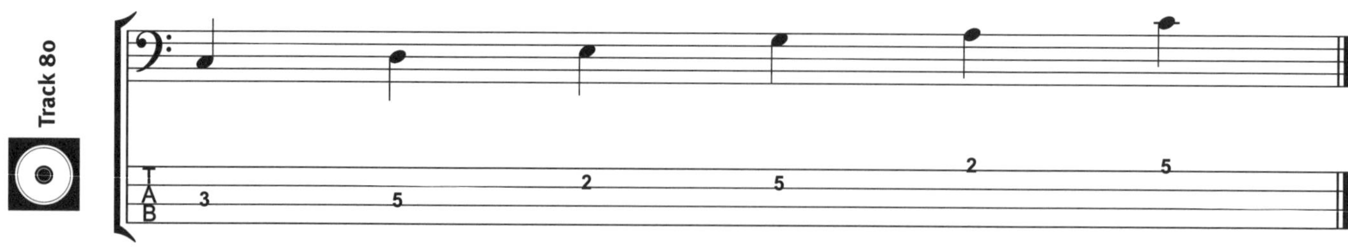

As I said, the pentatonic scale is derived from the major scale. The difference is that the fourth degree and the seventh degree have been removed – F and B in the case of the C major pentatonic scale. Play through the scale shown above a few times to get used to the sound. You'll notice it has a slight bluesy quality about it; this is partly what makes it so popular with guitarists.

PENTATONIC BOX SHAPES

Pentatonic scales are usually best used when you know how to play them at various points on the fretboard. The pentatonic scale can be broken down into five 'box' shapes that can be used when creating basslines or playing a solo. Each box shape will start on a different degree of the scale: the first on C, the second on D, and so on. These box shapes have formed the basis of many a rock guitar solo, and they're equally useful to bass players.

Here's the first box shape, starting on C:

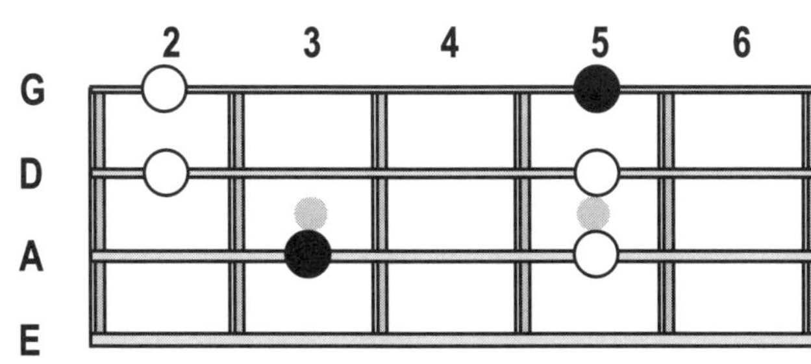

Here's the second box shape, starting on the second note of the pentatonic scale – the D:

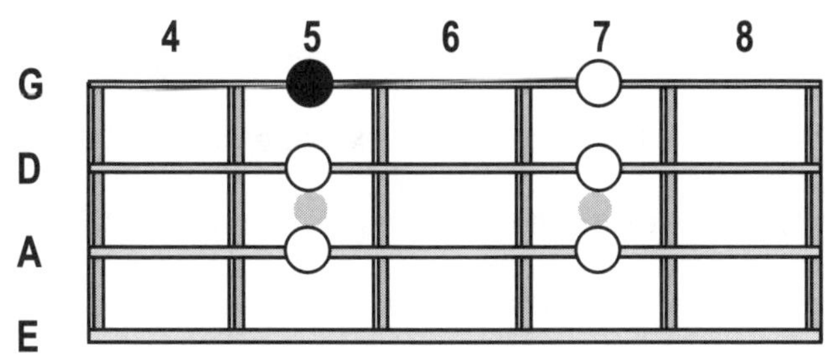

Here's the third shape. This one starts on the third degree of the scale, the E:

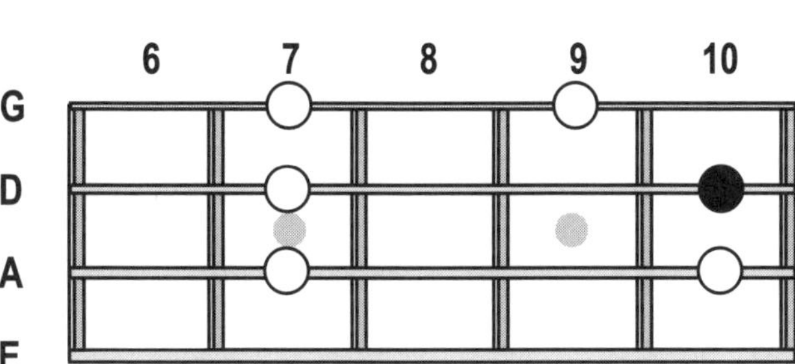

The fourth shape, starting on G:

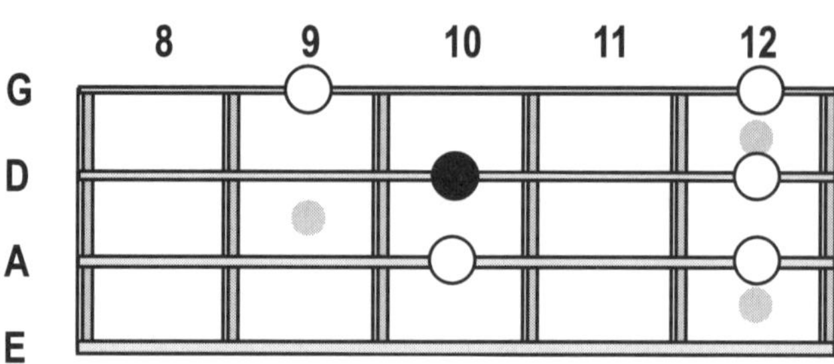

And finally the fifth box shape, starting on A:

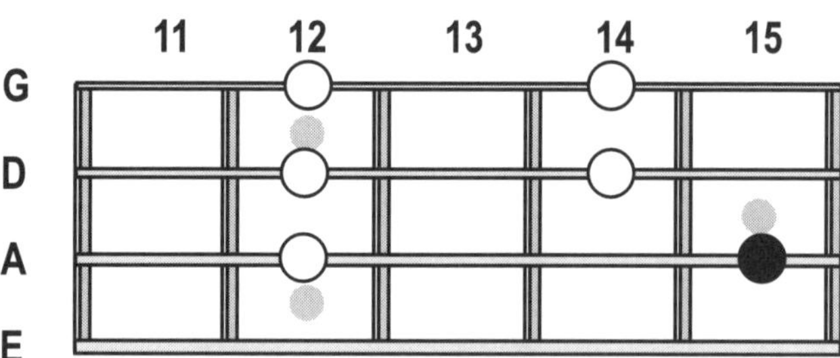

There are quite a few shapes to remember here, and it can be tough to do so. With this in mind, I've prepared an exercise which relates each box shape back to the root, C. This exercise has been recorded on the CD at a quick tempo that may prove tricky, so I suggest that you find a tempo you're comfortable with and stick to it. Then, as your playing progresses, you can increase speed.

Exercise 66

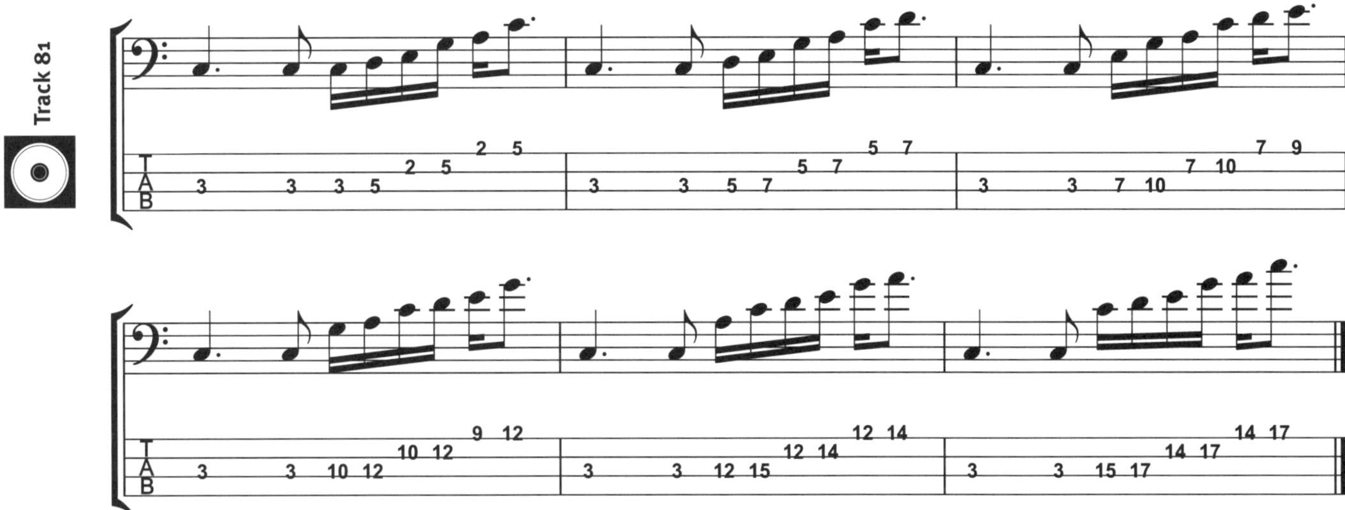

DAY 44 STUDY

1 Play through each box shape in turn until you've become familiar with all five.

2 Once you're happy with the individual shapes, work on Exercise 66.

DAY 45: 16th NOTES – PART 2

Your goal for Day 36 is to further your knowledge of 16th notes and to understand some new rhythmic groupings.

Back on Day 38, we began to look at 16th-note rhythms and how to go about reading them. There's no doubt that 16th-note-based rhythms are among the trickiest both to read and play, but if you study the following exercises carefully you should find things a little easier. Remember that you can also hear all of them recorded on the CD.

16th NOTES AND DOTTED EIGHTH NOTES

One of the most common rhythmic groupings involving a 16th note is the dotted eighth note and dotted 16th note. Since placing a dot after an eighth note will make it last for three quarters of a full beat, this gives you time for one 16th note before the next beat. This will fall on the 'la' of 'Co-ca Co-la.'

Exercise 67

You might it easier to think of this rhythm as playing on every beat and adding a quick 16th note just before each beat. Play through this exercise a few times in order to get comfortable with it.

Next, we're going to reverse this rhythm and have a 16th note followed by a dotted eighth note. This means you'll be playing on the first 'Co' and then again straight away on the 'ca', as illustrated below:

Exercise 68

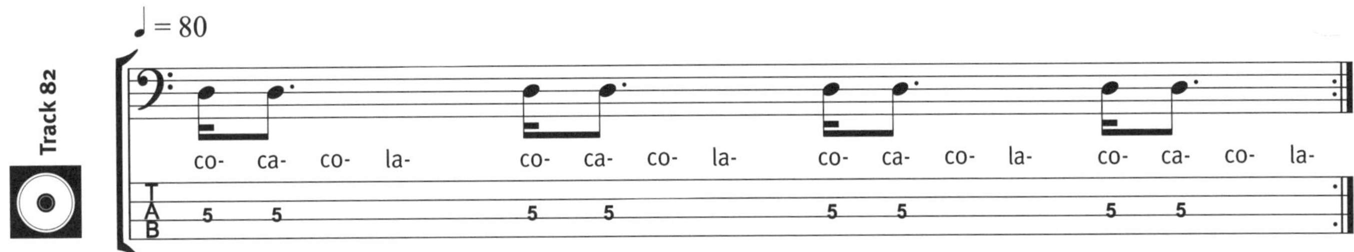

16th NOTES AND EIGHTH NOTE COMBINATIONS

It's also very common to combine an eighth not with two sixteenth notes. This can be done in the following two ways:

Exercise 69

This first method, above, creates a chugging rhythm that's popular in both pop and rock music. We'll now reverse this to have two 16ths followed by an eighth note:

Bass

Exercise 70

You'll hear that this sounds different again.

The final rhythm we'll look at today will be the 16th-note/eighth-note/16th-note rhythm. This looks quite unpleasant on paper, but once you know how it sounds, you shouldn't find it too difficult:

Exercise 71

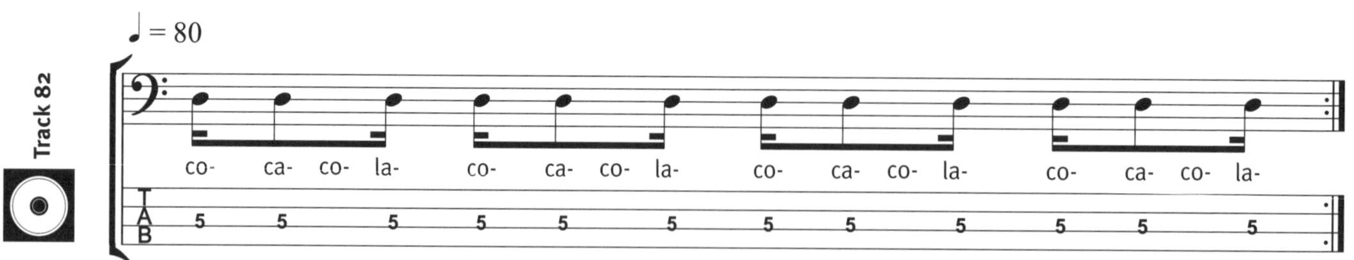

Remember that all of these rhythms will be mixed in with all the other rhythms explored so far. And now that you've looked at most of the different rhythmic combinations, you should have some idea of how a written rhythm should sound.

These 16th-note groupings are best approached slowly. Pay close attention to how they sound on the CD and how they're written.

DAY 45 STUDY

1 Practise all of the rhythmic groupings covered this week.

2 Look through any music books you might have lying around and look out for these rhythms. Try to work out how they should sound.

Bass

DAY 46: DYNAMICS

Your goal for Day 46 is to learn about dynamics and how they can benefit your playing.

When playing through a piece of music, you're able to give a much better performance if you know when to play quietly, when to play loudly, which notes to accent, etc. Dynamics are the indications that are written into a piece of music to tell you when to do these things. You won't see dynamics in tab; they're strictly for notated music. Today I'm going to introduce you to the main dynamics you should know and explain what they mean.

QUOTE FOR THE DAY

Remember that the number one job of a bassist is to make everyone else sound good!

– Dave Pomeroy, Nashville session bassist

The first dynamics we will look at are indications of volume. These are commonly seen at the beginning of a piece to tell you how loud to play, but they can also occur at any other point in a piece of music. All are based on Italian words, as you can see in the table below:

Dynamic	Full Name	Meaning
ff	fortissimo	very loud
f	forte	loud
mf	mezzo forte	medium loud
mp	mezzo piano	medium soft
p	piano	softly
pp	pianissimo	very softly

There are also directions that indicate when you should play gradually louder and quieter – *crescendo* and *diminuendo* respectively. These are also indicated by lines commonly known among musicians as *hairpins*.

Crescendo Diminuendo

Finally, you'll come across a number of performance directions for accenting notes, as well as shortening and extending notes. These are as follows:

- **Staccato** – Marked by a dot over the note, this means that the note is played very short and crisply. Staccato marks are sometimes written in place of shortening the notes actual value, as they are easier to read.

- **Tenuto** – Not nearly as common as staccato, tenuto means that the note should be held for its full value, and in some cases slightly longer than its true value.

- **Accents** – Accents are marked by a forward-pointing arrow over the note. This simply means that the note is to be accented (ie played a little harder than other notes).

Bass

You should make a point of looking back over all the basslines covered in this book and playing through the lines, paying attention to any performance directions that may have been included. You should also look through other music books to see dynamics and directions in use.

DAY 46 STUDY

1 Remember all of the dynamics talked about in this section. If possible, have someone test you on them.

2 What is a crescendo?

3 What should you do when you see the term 'tenuto'?

4 If you saw the dynamic *p* at the beginning of a piece, how would you play?

DAY 47: GHOST NOTES

Your goal for Day 47 is to learn about ghost notes.

You might well be wondering what on earth a ghost note is, although you've probably heard them many times before. A ghost note is a pitchless note which, when played, adds a percussive element to a bassline. Ghost notes are used extensively in slap bass, and we'll be looking at them again in that context in Week 8 of this course. However, ghost notes also work well in just about any kind of music, whether you're playing with your fingers or with a pick.

To play a ghost note, simply lift the fingers off the string slightly and play the string as normal. You should produce a note that's more of a *thud* than a pitched note. This is a ghost note, and you can hear me play a few examples on the CD. (Be careful where your fingers are placed when playing ghost notes. If you lift your fingers off the string slightly and are over certain frets, you'll produce a harmonic rather than a ghost note.)

Have a look at the simple exercise over the page, designed to help you to practise producing ghost notes. In this exercise below there are two bars of eighth notes. The first four are Es played as normal on the A string. The second four are ghost notes, played in the same way but by lifting the fretting fingers slightly to prevent a clear note from sounding. The second bar is the same, except that the fretted notes are Ds.

Bass

Exercise 72

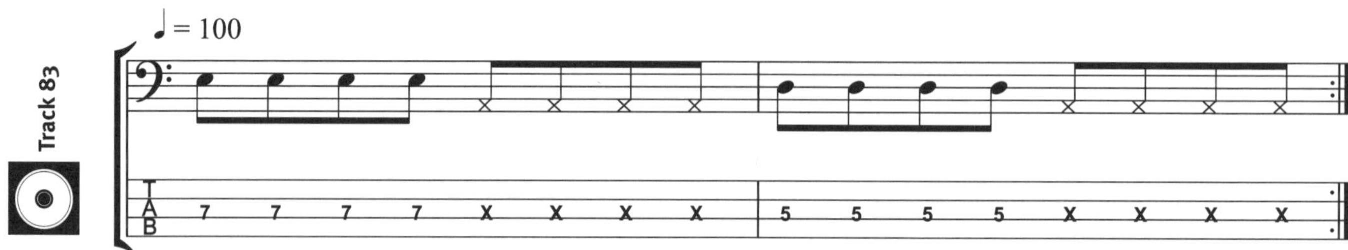

Note that ghost notes are notated as Xs on the strings on which they occur. Saying that, it doesn't make a great deal of difference which string you play them on, since a ghost note is a ghost note wherever you play it!

The best way to become accustomed to using ghost notes is to learn a few simple lines that incorporate them. To that end I've prepared two simple basslines that make use of ghost notes. Listen carefully to the CD – you'll hear that they give the line a slightly percussive feel and add a sense of movement.

Exercise 73

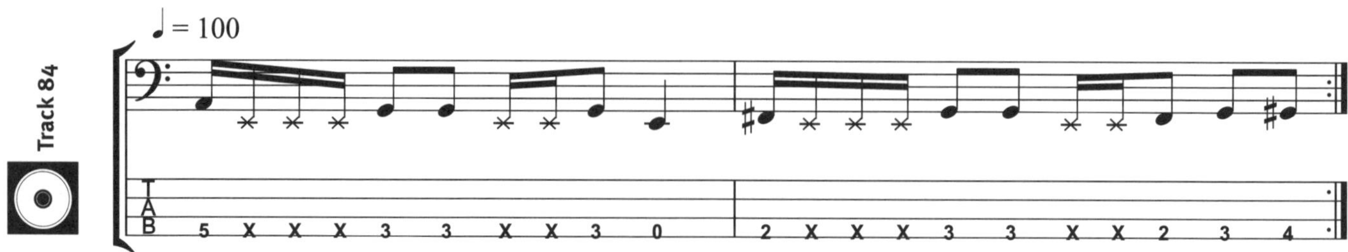

Exercise 74

It might take a little time to get the necessary left-hand coordination together for mixing ghost notes with regular pitches, but by working these exercises into your practice regime you should begin to hear results relatively quickly. Once you have these lines under your fingers, try to come up with some of your own.

If possible, listen to some of the following tracks to hear ghost notes in action:

Red Hot Chili Peppers: 'Funky Monks, If You Have To Ask'

Jaco Pastorius: 'Come On, Come Over'

Incubus: 'Battlestar Scralatchtika'

Rage Against The Machine: 'Bullet In The Head'

DAY 47 STUDY

1 Add the ghost-note exercises we've just looked at to your practice routine.

2 Listen to some of the songs mentioned above. It's always a good idea to hear a new techniques being used.

Bass

DAY 48: CORE TOPIC – REGGAE BASSLINES

Your goal for Day 48 is to learn two more reggae basslines, to follow on from the ones that you've been practising this week.

PRACTICAL EXERCISE

This line is much slower and has a slight swing feel to it. Note the sparseness of the line in the first four bars, which then gets slightly busier in the second half.

QUOTE FOR THE DAY

Stay in touch with the performance aspect of what you do and be prepared to apply that to every situation, live or recording. Be prepared.

– John Myung, Dream Theater

Exercise 75

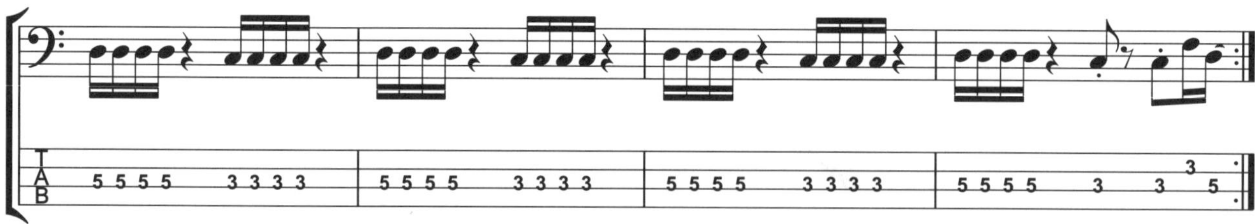

PRACTICAL EXERCISE

Here's another reggae line. Note again the use of triplets, this time at the end of the eight-bar cycle. Also worth a mention is the line in bars 5 and 7. Check out the octave-fifth-root descending part on beats 2 and 4 – another classic reggae move.

Exercise 76

Bob Marley: 'Could You Be Loved'

Bob Marley: 'Stir It Up'

Bob Marley: 'Three Little Birds'

The Police: 'Bed's Too Big Without You'

UB40: 'Red Red Wine'

Pete Tosh: 'Johnny B Goode'

Desmond Dekker: 'The Israelites'

Ken Boothe: 'Everything I Own'

Dawn Penn: 'You Don't Love Me (No, No, No)'

Dave And Ansel Collins: 'Double Barrel'

DAY 48 STUDY

1 Practise all of the reggae basslines you learnt today and earlier in the week.

2 Be sure that you understand everything covered this week. Tomorrow is test day again!

Bass

DAY 49

WEEK 7 TEST

Today is your seventh test day. As before, you should complete this test before moving on. Everything you need to know was covered in the previous week.

---

1 Who, with his band The Wailers, was one of the leading figures in reggae music?

2 Name some of the characteristics of reggae music.

3 How does the major pentatonic scale differ from the major scale?

4 How many box shapes are derived from the pentatonic scale?

5 Write the correct names beneath these two performance directions:

6. What does *ff* mean?

7 What does *tenuto* mean?

8 What would you write if you wanted a piece of music to be performed 'medium loud?'

9 What is a ghost note?

10 What are the benefits of using ghost notes in your playing?

TIMED EXERCISE

Finally, her's another reggae bassline for you to study. You should aim to be able to play this one within 30 minutes.

WEEK 8

OVERVIEW

Welcome to the final week of your Crash Course in bass guitar. This week we'll be finishing off all of the topics we've been looking at, although there will still be plenty of scope for your own continued study. We'll also be taking a look at funk music and having some fun with the basics of slap-bass technique. Here's a full breakdown of what we'll be looking at in the coming week:

- **Core Topic: Funk Music** – This is the final core topic. As usual, we'll look briefly at the history of funk and learn four typical funk basslines.

- **The Minor Pentatonic Scale** – Now that you know what the major pentatonic is, it's time to look at the minor version.

- **Music Notation** – This week we'll take a look at the triplet, and we'll look at how eighth-note and quarter-note triplets are written and played.

- **Slap Bass** – Slap bass is a vital element in the funk style, so it's only fitting that we take an introductory look at it this week!

Bass

DAY 50: CORE TOPIC – FUNK MUSIC

Your goal for Day 50 is to learn about funk music and to play some typical funk basslines.

Funk music evolved out of R&B music in the late '60s thanks to artists like James Brown, Maceo Parker and Sly Stone. Many bass players were responsible for the bass guitar's growing contribution to the style, none more so than Larry Graham, who single-handedly invented the slap technique that became synonymous with funk music. Funk has a undeniable groove and is great fun to play – as you'll hear when you play these lines.

QUOTE FOR THE DAY

What I liked about Jamerson was the way he was playing melodies rather than just root notes. That kind of polyphonic idea appealed to me on the bass, as opposed to just a supporting role. – *Jack Bruce*

PRACTICAL EXERCISE

This is based around a repeating one-bar classic funk-style figure. The staccato marks on the E and G of each bar will help you to capture the funk feel. This line is quite tricky but features a lot of repetition.

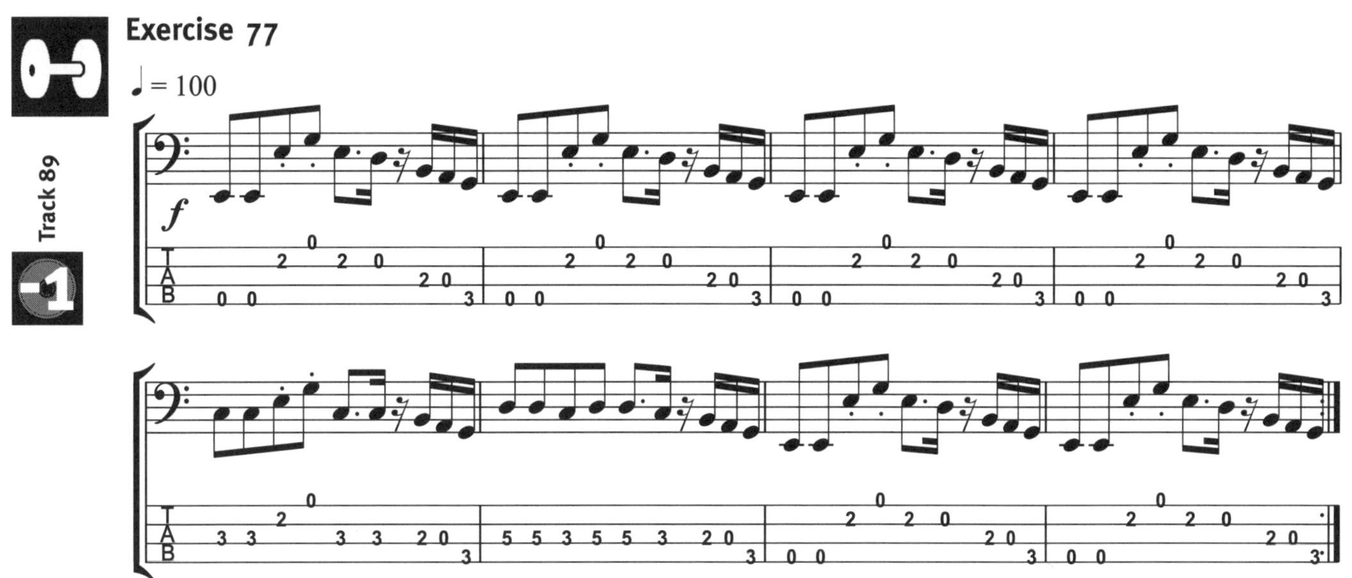

Bass

PRACTICAL EXERCISE

A much more sparse line. The note choices throughout this line are pure funk. The great thing about this line is that it's quite simple and sounds great. This is often the case with funk music, where a line doesn't have to be complex to groove.

Exercise 78

DAY 50 STUDY

1 Practise the three funk lines we've just looked at. Continue to work on them throughout the week.

DAY 51: INTRODUCTION TO SLAP BASS

Your goals for Day 51 are:

- To understand the basics of the slap technique;
- To learn some very simple slap lines.

QUOTE FOR THE DAY

I fell in love with it because there are so many things you can do on a bass. You can play with your fingers, you can slap, or you can use a pick. It just seems so awesome to me. I play a whole bunch of Primus stuff, which is playing bass to a whole new level. You're turning bass into a percussion instrument. Bass is the greatest thing in the world!

– Paul Thomas, Good Charlotte

Slap bass is one of those styles that you see/hear and just have to try – whether you stick with it or not! It's been around for almost 30 years now (on the electric bass, at least), and most players know at least a few slap lines. While it can be tricky to get started with this technique, it's not as hard as you might think, and it doesn't take an unreasonably long time to start getting results. Since we've been looking at funk lines this week, I thought it only fitting that we have an introductory look at slap bass, too – after all, it's most commonly associated with funk music, although it can be used in other styles too. Slap bass is actually deserving of an entire book in itself, and many have been written on the subject. With that in mind – and in light of the fact that, if you're reading this, you've probably been playing for only a couple of months – here's a quick look at the basics.

THE THUMB

The first part of slap bass that we need to look at is how to slap the strings with the thumb. As you'll see in the photograph over the page, the thumb is best placed to hit the string if it's aligned to be parallel to it. This means that you don't have to wear your bass too low (although you'll experience difficulties with the technique if you wear the bass down around your knees!), and you'll find it easier to hit strings other than the E this way.

You should be striking the string with the side of the thumb, on the side of the knuckle bone. Try slapping the open E string – you can hear on the CD how it should sound. This will be tricky to begin with, but hang in there and remember that anything is possible. It's just down to practice!

Now try hitting some of the other strings. In the next exercise you'll be slapping just the E, A and D strings. Why not the G? Well, the G is very thin in comparison, and it doesn't sound that great when slapped. Instead, you'll be 'popping' this

string – but we'll look at that a little later. You'll see that slaps are indicated by a letter t, for 'thumb.'

Exercise 79

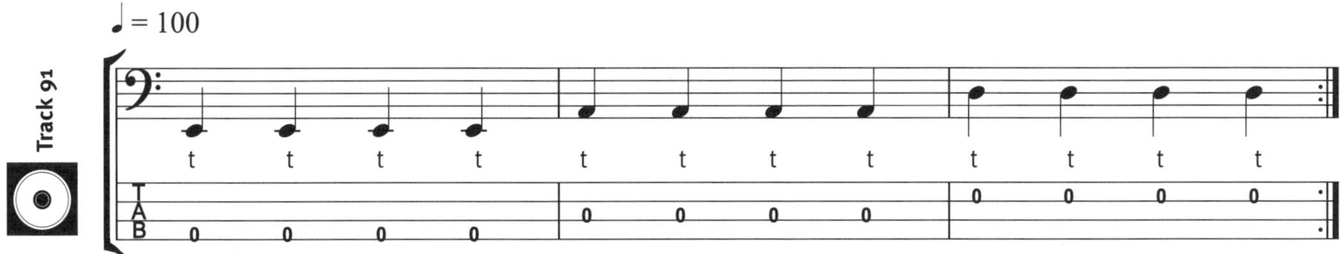

Depending on how you got on with that last exercise, you might want to stop and keep working on your technique. If in doubt, refer to the photograph opposite.

Now let's try a similar exercise. This time we're going to incorporate some fretted notes as well. For the moment, we;re going to stick to notes on the E string, since this is the easiest string to slap:

Exercise 80

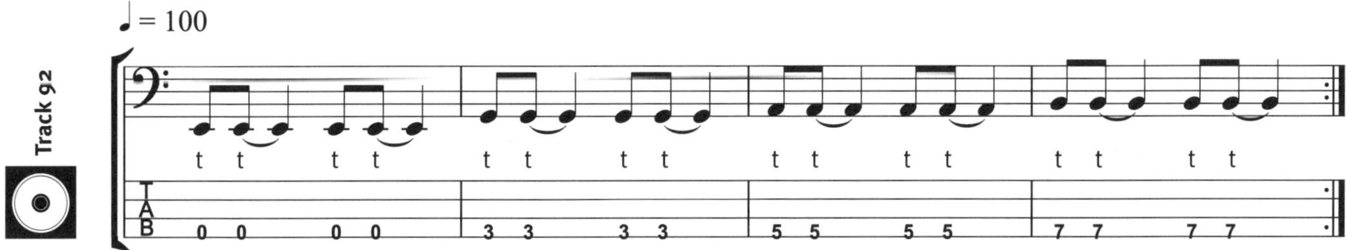

MUTING

Muting is vital when playing with the slap technique. You'll recall that muting with the left hand was covered back on Day 17. Today we're going to employ those same techniques to shorten the notes in the previous exercise. Remember, to shorten an open string note, simply rest your fingers on the string to stop it ringing; to shorten a fretted note, lift your fingers slightly, but not all the way off. You can, of course, hear this on the CD.

Exercise 81

I think that's enough for one day! I realise that we haven't looked at much actual music today, but I think it's important for you to be as comfortable as possible with the basics before you think about getting too adventurous. We'll look at slapping again in a few days' time.

I recommend checking out the following tracks:

Red Hot Chili Peppers: 'Aeroplane', 'Naked In The Rain', 'Backwoods'

Rage Against The Machine: 'Take The Power Back'

Stanley Clarke: 'Lopsy Lu', 'Hot Fun'

Level 42: 'Lessons In Love', 'Mr Pink'

Stu Hamm: 'Sexually Active', 'Country Music', 'Black Ice'

Victor Wooten: 'You Can't Hold No Groove', 'Me And My Bass Guitar'

DAY 51 STUDY

1. Practise the slap exercises in this section.
2. Investigate some well-known slap players. Listen to as much slap technique as you can!

DAY 52: TRIPLETS

Your goal for Day 52 is to learn about triplets – how they sound and how to read them.

This is the last rhythmic variation that we'll be looking at in this book. We've covered pretty much all of the basic rhythms, and you should by now have some idea of how music is written. While at this point you probably won't be able to read music fluently, all of the ingredients to help you on your way are within these pages.

I've saved this particular rhythmic variation until last because it's written slightly differently from the others. Basically, the triplet comprises three equally spaced notes in the space of two. Using the rhythms we've seen so far, it's possible to cover many rhythmic possibilities, but none of these allow you to play three equal notes per beat. There's no mathematically correct way to notate a triplet, so to speak, so the three notes are grouped together and topped off with a number 3, indicating that the notes are to be played as triplets.

Here's a bar of eighth-note triplets, the most common form. There are three notes on each beat, and so in a bar of 4/4 time it's possible to have 12 triplet notes. Check out the CD to hear how they sound. (You'll have seen and played these triplets in the reggae basslines from Week 7 as well.)

You'll probably agree that they sound quite normal. You may even be wondering what all the fuss was about!

Here's a line that incorporates these eighth note triplets:

Exercise 82

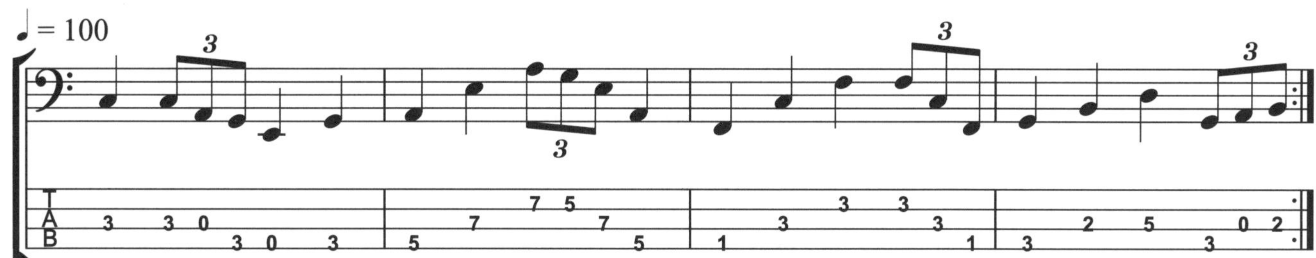

The second kind of triplet we're going to look at is the quarter-note triplet – that is, three equally spaced notes in the space of two quarter notes. Have a listen to the example below to hear how they sound. I've used them in conjunction with regular eighth notes so you hear them in context:

Exercise 83

There are other types of triplet as well: the 16th-note triplet (really nasty!) and the half-note triplet. Both are less common than these two, and are really beyond the scope of this book.

My advice to you now is to study some more printed music. Be on the lookout for triplets now as well. I find it good practice to sit and study music in this way, and imagine in my head how the rhythms will sound. By practising all of the rhythm exercises in this book, you should be off to a great start. Good luck.

DAY 52 STUDY

1 Practise the triplet exercises shown this week.

2 Go back and look at the reggae lines from Week 7. Triplets are important in the reggae style, and it will be good for you to now hear them in context and be able recognise them for what they are.

DAY 53: THE MINOR PENTATONIC SCALE

Your goal for Day 53 is to learn the A minor pentatonic scale and look at the shapes derived from it.

Having looked at the major pentatonic scale on Day 44, you should hopefully be able to see how pentatonics can be very useful to us as bass players. Today's lesson focuses on the minor pentatonic, which is just as useful. The minor pentatonic, like the major, contains only five notes (six including the octave) and essentially is a natural minor scale without the second or sixth degrees. Here are the notes of the A natural minor and the A minor pentatonic for you to compare:

A Natural Minor: A B C D E F G A

A Minor Pentatonic: A C D E G A

Like we did with the major pentatonic, we're going to look at a different box shapes, starting from each note of the fretboard. After you've had a look at these box shapes, you'll find an exercise that will allow you to practise them while referring back to the root note.

Here's the first box shape, from the root note, A:

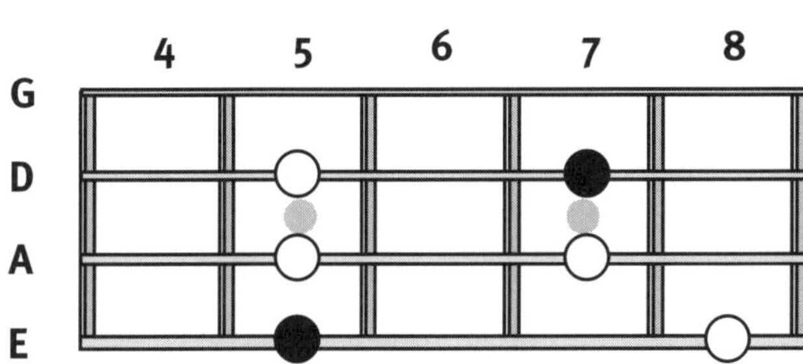

Bass

Here's the second box shape, starting from the second note of the scale, C:

6 7 8 9 10
G
D
A
E

Here's the third box shape, starting from the third note, D:

8 9 10 11 12
G
D
A
E

Here's the fourth box pattern, starting from the fourth note, E:

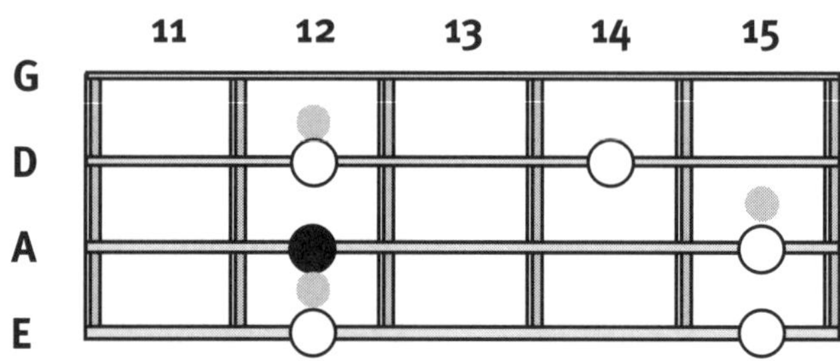

Finally, here's the fifth box shape, starting on the fifth note, G:

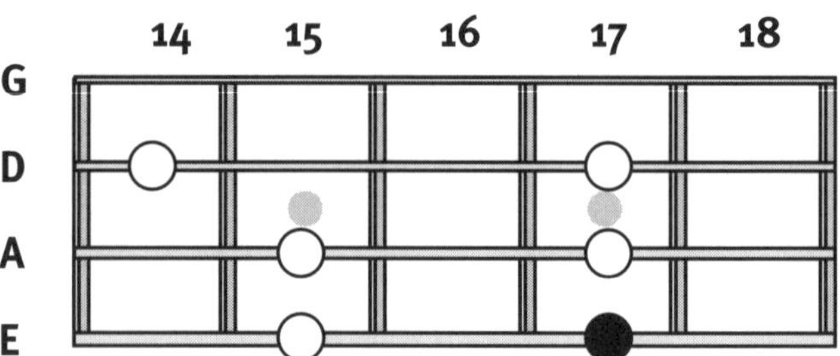

Remember that you can move most of these box shapes across to start on the corresponding note on the A string. This may make them easier to play.

There are quite a few shapes to remember here, and it can be tough to do so. With that in mind I've prepared an exercise which relates each box shape back to the root, A. There are six boxes in the exercise below, the last being a repeat of the first box only an octave higher. Again, the CD version of this exercise was recorded quite fast, but you should set your own comfortable tempo and progress from there.

Exercise 84

Again, once you have these shapes under your fingers, I suggest you practise them in random order in order to really get the scale under your fingers. You may want to explore different positions for them, too – for instance, many of the patterns could be moved to start from equivalent notes on the E string instead of the A.

Finally, remember that major and minor scales are related – and so too are major and minor pentatonics. For example, C major pentatonic contains the notes C, D, E,

G, A and C, while its relative minor – A minor – contains the notes A, C, D, E, G and A. Same notes, different order. Therefore, by practising the C major pentatonic box shapes, you're also practising the A minor pentatonic shapes, just in a different order. You can even compare these box shapes to the ones we looked at back on Day 44 – you'll see that they're the same, but in a different order. This might be a little difficult to understand now, but with time you'll begin to see the relationships.

DAY 53 STUDY

1 Play through the A minor pentatonic scale a few times in order to become acquainted with the sound.

2 Play through each box shape in turn in order to get your fingers acquainted with each one.

3 Once you're happy with the individual shapes, work on Exercise 84.

DAY 54: MORE SLAP BASS

Your goals for Day 54 are:

- To learn a little more about slap bass;
- To learn and practise some further slap bass exercises.

Back on day 51 we looked at how to use the thumb and the ways in which you need to strike the string to produce the slap sound. Today, we'll look at the left hand in a little more detail, in particular the first and second fingers, which are used for 'popping' the top strings.

Track 95

THE LEFT HAND

The left hand plays a vital role in slap bass. Last time we looked at the left-hand muting technique, which can be used to shorten notes, making them staccato. The left hand can also be used to produce notes on its own, most commonly ghost notes. (Hopefully you'll remember our old friend the ghost note from day 47.) To produce these with the left hand, simply strike the string with the insides of the fingers. The image over the page demonstrates how this is done, and you can hear how it should sound on Track 95 of the CD. Used in conjunction with thumb slaps, it's possible to build up fast slap lines by co-ordinating the two hands.

Take a look at the following exercise, which requires you to alternate thumb slaps and left-hand ghost notes. Remember that your thumb doesn't slap the string for the left hand notes; these are produced entirely by the left hand, indicated by the letters lh.

Exercise 85

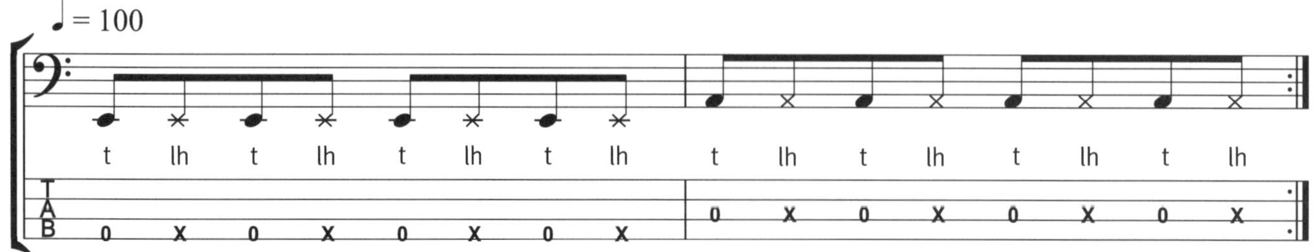

A good analogy for this type of technique is drumming with your hands on a tabletop. In fact, that's a good way to practise this exercise without your bass! We'll look at a few lines that incorporate the left hand technique at the end of this section.

Track 96

THE POP

The top string, the G (and quite often the D), is usually 'popped' by one of the fingers rather than slapped with the thumb. This will be a familiar sound to anyone who has heard slap bass before – it's that final, funky ingredient! To pop the G string, hook the tip of your finger underneath it, as shown in the photograph below, and pluck it. You can afford to be quite aggressive with it, but be careful that you don't start breaking strings! You can hear how the pop should sound on the accompanying CD.

The pop will almost always be combined with thumb slaps. Below is a straightforward slap-and-pop exercise based around octaves (a very common choice, as far as popped notes go). Note that pops are indicated by the letter p.

Exercise 86

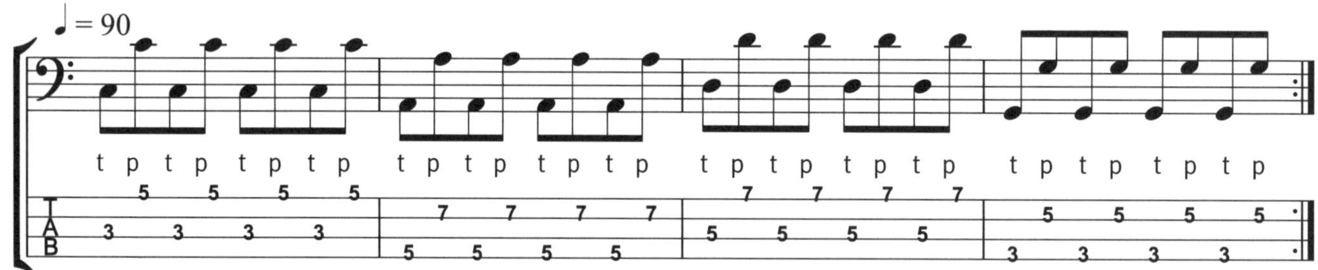

We've now looked at the three basic elements of slap bass. There's really not a lot more to it than that. The rest is just down to practice!

Remember, it might take a while to start getting results with the slap technique, but it really is all down to practice. Everything you need to know is shown in this week's lessons and on the CD.

DAY 54 STUDY

1 Work on all aspects of the slap technique introduced this week.

2 Study the basslines introduced today. Don't worry if you don't get them right in one day; use them as part of an ongoing practice routine.

DAY 55: CORE TOPIC – FUNK BASSLINES

Your goal for Day 55 is to learn another two funk basslines, so I'll leave you with two final funk parts to look at.

PRACTICAL EXERCISE

This is classic funk line based around a repeating two-chord progression that's very common in funk music. The great thing about funk is that it's all about the feeling, the groove. Consequently, chord progressions and instrumental parts don't necessarily have to be very complex at all.

QUOTE FOR THE DAY

I think what keeps the fire going is that it's about where you're going and not resting on what you have accomplished.

– *John Myung, Dream Theater*

Exercise 87

Bass

PRACTICAL EXERCISE

Here's another line based around very static harmony. This one has a funk-swing to it – you'll see what I mean when you hear it. It looks like a bit of a nightmare on paper, but it shouldn't prove too difficult with a little practice. Note the octave figure on the first beat of each bar – this is a useful trick with funk music. Also worth a mention is the bluesy line in bars 4 and 8.

Exercise 88

Track 98

Finally, to further your knowledge of funk music, I recommend the following tracks:

James Brown: 'Get Up, I Feel Like Being A Sex Machine'

James Brown: 'Cold Sweat'

Red Hot Chili Peppers: 'Aeroplane'

Red Hot Chili Peppers: 'Mellowship Slinky In B Major'

Average White Band: 'Pick Up The Pieces'

Average White Band: 'Cut The Cake'

Stevie Wonder: 'I Wish'

The Brand New Heavies: 'Back To Love'

Jamiroquai: 'Hooked Up'

Kool And The Gang: 'Jungle Boogie'

DAY 55 STUDY

1 Practise all of the funk basslines you learnt today and earlier in the week.

2 Be sure you understand everything covered in this chapter. Tomorrow is your final test day!

Bass

DAY 56

WEEK 8 TEST

Today is your eighth and final test day. Everything you need to know to pass this test was covered in the previous week's lessons.

QUOTE FOR THE DAY

I don't think musicians ever really retire. You just fall off your perch!

– *Jack Bruce*

1 Name some of the characteristics of funk music.

2 What is the best way to slap a string with the thumb?

3 What are the three basic elements of slap bass?

4 What are the first and second fingers commonly used for in slap bass?

5 What is a triplet?

6 Why is it necessary to write a number 3 over a triplet?

7 How many eighth-note triplets is it possible to have in a bar of 4/4?

8 How many quarter-note triplets is it possible to have in a bar of 4/4?

9 How does the minor pentatonic scale differ from the minor scale?

10 A minor pentatonic is related to which major scale?

TIMED EXERCISE

Finally, here's another new funk bassline for you to study. You should aim to be able to play this one within 30 minutes.

Bass

Bass

Bass

Bass

Bass

TAB

TAB

TAB

TAB

TAB